The
Spirit
of
Judgment

The Spirit Of Judgment

WATCHMAN NEE

Translated from the Chinese

Christian Fellowship Publishers, Inc.
New York

ISBN 0-935008-63-2

Available from the Publishers at:

11515 Allecingie Parkway
Richmond, Virginia 23235

PRINTED IN U.S.A.

TRANSLATOR'S PREFACE

People do not like to think of judgment, but "the Lord is known by the judgment which he executeth" (Ps. 9.16 AV). The psalmist "sing[s] of mercy and judgment" (Ps. 101.1 AV). He asks the Lord to teach him of His judgment (Ps. 119.108 AV), and to quicken him according to His judgment (Ps. 119.149 AV). He considers those blessed who keep judgment and do righteousness at all times (Ps. 106.3 AV). May we therefore be corrected in our mental concept and enter into the spirit of judgment so that God may be justified and we may be perfected.

The present volume is composed of three parts. The first comprises notes of the messages on the Spirit of Judgment which Watchman Nee delivered in February, 1942 at a seven-day conference in Shanghai, China. Their full text has never been published and is now lost. However, these notes—taken by Dr. C. H. Yu—have been miraculously preserved and are now being translated and published into English.

The second part offers three of the now well-known 52 basic lessons for believers which the author gave during a series of training sessions for workers held at Mount Kuling, near Foochow, China, in 1948.* These

---

*The reader should be aware that besides the three lessons alluded to above, one lesson (Sickness) was translated into English and incorporated into the chapter entitled Sickness (Volume 3, Part 10, Chapter 2) found in Watchman Nee, *The Spiritual Man*, 3 vols. (New York: Christian Fellowship Publishers, 1968); while almost three lessons (on the Kingdom, the Lord's Second Coming, and Occupation) had not been translated and published into English earlier because of their potentially controversial nature due to wide differences of opinion held among believers concerning these three subjects. Yet we feel these views should now be presented to all who love the truth of God. Their inclusion here is not aimed at forcing upon but rather at stirring up believers to at least consider them seriously before the Lord.

The third part of the volume gathers together a number of messages given by the author at different times and places during his fruitful ministry and which have not been translated and published in English heretofore. They cover a wide range of subjects — from the righteousness of God to the helpmeet of Christ, yet they all unite in presenting the fullness of the salvation of our God.

May God use this book to bring all who read it into a deeper knowledge of, and more consistent walk with, the Lord Jesus Christ.

---

all of the 52 lessons (48 in number), have previously been translated into English, re-arranged and variously grouped together into six volumes, and published under the general title of the *Basic Lesson Series* (New York: Christian Fellowship Publishers, 1972–75). The six individual volume titles in this series are as follows: *A Living Sacrifice* (1972), *The Good Confession* (1973), *Assembling Together* (1973), *Not I But Christ* (1974), *Do All to the Glory of God* (1974), and *Love One Another* (1975).—*Translator*

CONTENTS

Scripture quotations are from the
American Standard Version of the Bible
(1901), unless otherwise indicated.

PART ONE

THE SPIRIT OF JUDGMENT*

*Being notes—taken down by Dr. C. H. Yu—of the author's messages spoken at a February 1942 conference in Shanghai, China.

1 | Known by His Judgment

Jehovah hath made himself known, he hath executed judgment. (Ps. 9.16)

When thy judgments are in the earth, the inhabitants of the world learn righteousness. (Is. 26.9)

In the day when God shall judge the secrets of men, according to my gospel, by Jesus Christ. (Rom. 2.16)

And I saw a great white throne, and him that sat upon it, from whose face the earth and the heaven fled away; and there was found no place for them. And I saw the dead, the great and the small, standing before the throne; and books were opened: and another book was opened, which is the book of life: and the dead were judged out of the things which were written in the books, according to their works. And the sea gave up the dead that were in it: and death and Hades gave up the dead that were in them: and they were judged every man according to their works. And death and Hades were cast into the lake of fire. This is the second death, even the lake of fire. And

if any was not found written in the book of life, he was
cast into the lake of fire. (Rev. 20.11-15)

Ordinarily we do not like to hear the word "judgment" for it does not seem to connote any spiritual help
and appears to be too negative. Yet aside from creation, God has not undertaken a work greater than judgment. The first thing He does is creation; but the last
is judgment. Without judgment God's purpose of creation cannot be arrived at. So that in His plan His judgment is *con*structive, not *de*structive. Future judgment
enables God to achieve His goal of creation. As we
know, creation is to manifest God's purpose; but the
devil, sin and the flesh soon thereafter came in. How,
then, can His purpose ever be realized if there is no
judgment?

Why is judgment necessary? Let us see that the very
last work of God is judgment, after which He has no
need to do anything else. On the seventh day God rested,
for the work of creation was finished. After judgment
the tabernacle of God, we are told, shall dwell among
men forever (Rev. 21.3ff.). Whereas the work of creation does not insure that sin will never enter again, judgment guarantees that sin will forever be gone. While
the work of creation fails to prevent the world from
rebelling, judgment makes certain that hereafter there
will be no more rebellion. God's judgment guarantees
no more sin. Judgment has the power to drive away sin.
So judgment has subjective uses in relation to us. At
least in three areas God will accomplish His will through
judgment:

(1) *Judgment glorifies God himself.* The judge is glorified according to the judgment he gives. The way sin is judged expresses the kind of person handing down the judgment. The deeper the hate for sin, the severer the judgment. Hence God's judgment reveals what kind of God He is. Through judgment God sanctifies himself.

Moses was the meekest of all men. The children of Israel murmured against both God and Moses. Moses might have appeared to have had every right to lose his temper at that time by his having said, "You rebels!", and by his having struck the rock with the rod for water. Yet let us recall that God had said to Moses to *speak* to the rock for water. So God said to Moses, "Because you do not sanctify Me before the eyes of the children of Israel, you cannot enter Canaan." Why in this instance was judgment executed upon Moses? Because otherwise, the children of Israel would never have known whether it had been God or Moses who lost the temper. But through this judgment upon Moses, all Israelites knew that it was Moses and not God who lost his temper. It seems ironic that the *murmurers* could enter Canaan, but the *reprover* could not. Nevertheless God was glorified. By Moses having been judged, God's glory was thus preserved.

Let us see that God hates sin. Cheap forgiveness may cause people to forget He is holy. If He were always lenient towards the children of Israel, the latter might never know God. When Moses was judged, everybody realized that God is holy. For God can vindicate His holiness at any time he wishes. (If people kick against judgment and wish it to pass away, they may be released;

but then, what would they say about God?) Therefore, let us declare to God, It is right for You to lay Your hand on me. (Our problem lies in how we can glorify God. Suppose we are judged when we lose our temper; will we gladly accept judgment in order to glorify God?)

During the Northern Conquest in China in the early nineteen thirties, I committed an unrighteous act. I then became sick. Though I prayed, I was not heard. I was rather surprised that God did not hear me. Until one day I saw and mused: You have committed the unrighteous thing; what will all those brethren who know about it think and say, and what kind of God is He if you are not judged? If indeed my being judged will cause people to fear You, I would rather enter into death. So on that day I saw that by His judging me, God would be more glorified than by His answering my prayer. In this instance, my being healed would glorify God less than my being judged. So that judgment gives God the purest glory.

(2) *Judgment exposes all hidden things, manifests the true character, and causes us to know ourselves.* People do not know themselves; they are deceived. One day God shall judge the world and manifest all the hidden things. He who will be the most surprised is each person's own self, for no one truly knows himself. Judgment will cause us to know our true character. Whatever has been hidden from us will be exposed on that day. Hence judgment is a great revelation, not only revealing God but also revealing what kind of person we are. "Yea, I judge not mine own self," said Paul; instead, he will wait "until the Lord come[s], who will both bring

to light the hidden things of darkness, and make manifest the counsels of the hearts" (1 Cor. 4.3,5).

Only a fool would trust in himself. However great your revelation is and however much your dealing is, you should not become over-confident. Paul was a man of revelation, yet he dared not judge himself. Judgment is a great exposure. In hell, there will be all kinds of people except the proud (pride is the sin that Satan commits). For the proud can continue on till they reach the great white throne of judgment. But then and there they will not be able to be proud anymore. Hence Paul declares that every knee shall bow and every tongue shall confess that Jesus is the Lord. This sin of pride will not be continued. Sooner or later all shall know themselves. Though you may not confess Jesus as Lord today, one day you *will* confess Him as such. On that day you will be dethroned and will acknowledge yourself to be but dust.

(3) *Before God judgment has a great effect — that is to say, it puts an end to sin.* Whatever sin it may be, it ceases after its being judged. The world is so terrible for it is filled with all kinds of sin. Sin advances so rapidly that nothing seems to be able to stop it. Preaching the gospel is one way to stop sin, but more people are being born into the world than are being saved into the kingdom. The number of people born in one day exceeds the number of souls being saved in one year. (It would almost appear as if the gospel, the cross, the church, the New Covenant have all failed; yet we know God does not use these but judgment to ultimately solve the problem of sin.) The entire problem of sin will be

resolved in judgment. What the gospel cannot stop, judgment will. Whatever has not been terminated will be terminated by judgment. Judgment is God's great cleansing day. It is the day in which sin is finally ended in this world. It is by far the best day, for on that day God shall reign. God will come among men and judge and destroy all which men and the devil have done. He will bring in the new. The world which came into being in the day of Genesis shall be purified in the day of Revelation 20. It will be renewed, and God shall be satisfied. The church, however, must submit to God's judgment today.

2 | Redeemed with Judgment

I will turn my hand upon thee, and thoroughly purge
away thy dross, and will take away all thy alloy; and I will
restore thy judges as at the first, and thy counsellors as
at the beginning: afterward thou shalt be called The city
of righteousness, a faithful town. Zion shall be redeemed
with justice, and her converts with righteousness. (Is.
1.25-27 mg.)

"Zion shall be redeemed with judgment" (Darby's
translation). Sin is Satan's challenge. It is unquestionably a difficult problem for God to solve. We often
mistakenly deem redemption to be God's answer, but
redemption is only part of the answer. The final
response by God to sin is judgment. Our darkened
thought considers judgment to be useless, because to
us judgment is Hades, the lake of fire, suffering, and
so forth. We fail to believe that in judgment lies God's
power. Though judgment is destructive, it also possesses

the greatest constructive power. Since God is willing to answer Satan's challenge with judgment, we are forced to conclude that it must be a very good answer. Whether we understand or not, judgment answers the challenge completely (for whatever God does is always perfect). Our mistake is, that every time we think of judgment we think of punishment; but God takes no delight in punishing men. Judgment has its other use besides punishment: "Jesus said, For judgment came I into this world" (John 9.39).

In the Old Testament period you will notice several times that God used judgment to answer the problem of sin. For example, in the day of Genesis 3 there was a garden. God created man and placed him in Eden in order to have fellowship with him. But sin came into the picture. The serpent spoke but once and man immediately fell into sin. Yet as sin came in, God answered with judgment by driving man out of Eden so that he might not sin in the garden the second time. The garden was thereafter guarded. So judgment was God's counterattack. It served as the answer to the entry of sin.

Later, during the time of Noah, men became ever more wicked. So God prepared the ark on the one hand and judgment on the other. Both the ark and the flood came from God. The ark offered redemption whereas the flood judged the world. The ark saved Noah, but the flood saved the world. If salvation had been restricted to the persons in the ark alone, it would not have been great enough. The world as well as men must be saved. Redemption came upon both men and the world. And God saved both. In like manner today, He will establish the kingdom as well as the church. He works to have the church first and then He shall have the kingdoms of this world to become His kingdom. There will indeed be judgment, but judgment will come to purify the world from its evil.

During the time of Exodus there was still another instance of judgment. God's people were living in Goshen, Pharaoh was on the throne, and God's people fell into the hands of the idol-worshiping Egyptians. Deliverance of God's people finally came through the blood; and the destroying Angel weakened the Egyptians by killing their firstborn. The sacrificial lamb enabled God's people to leave Egypt. They crossed the Rea Sea, but the Egyptians could not go through. So that we can see redemption on the one hand and judgment on the other. The Egyptians were drowned and buried in the Red Sea. Their power was broken by judgment. As a matter of fact, judgment destroys every opposing force.

We can also find many instances of judgment during the period of the book of Judges. As the children of Israel would fail, God would raise up judges to defeat their oppressors. Now these judges were those who from time to time judged God's enemies. Every time sin became a problem, God reacted with judgment. So that when God arose, sin was stopped. Judgment truly cleanses.

Likewise in the New Testament we find a series of judgments pictured for us in the form of seven seals, seven trumpets and seven vials. These are told of in the book of Revelation. The book of Revelation quite simply glides over the millennium, and most likely because a thousand-year-period cannot be considered as being so long. It is merely something that is presented as happening in between judgments. Doubtless, the emphasis there is on judgment. During the thousand years, people are going to learn righteousness, not grace. Learning righteousness is the same as learning judgment because judgment manifests God's righteousness.

Finally, we see in Revelation that God shall use one last judgment to finish off Satan. Judgment is based on authority, not on power. God puts the devil as well as men under judgment that they all might know He is God. Judgment weakens sin; and it secures victory for God. Send Thy judgment, O Lord, unto victory! (see Matt. 12.20)

If we were to stop at this point in our discussion, all might appear to be objective doctrines. But we know the burning fire is also the enlightening fire. We may have sinned and yet we are not aware of it because we live in the natural. We may continue living on for five or ten years without truly knowing ourselves. One day God has mercy upon us and enlightens us with the light of judgment (for light burns and sin is discontinued). Only when we live in darkness may we live our natural lives peacefully. But once light comes, we can live that way no longer.

We may not know why in future judgment men will hide in caves and call upon the mountains and rocks to cover them. But we do know that in judgment whatever is covered is uncovered. God sees us through and through, but we do not know ourselves. In the day of judgment, however, we shall see the things which God had found in us. We cannot hide anything from God, yet we still want to cover ourselves. So we as it were call upon the mountains to hide us. Such seeing unsettles us. It gives us great pain because we know we have sinned. Yet this knowledge also dries up the sin in us. In searching out sin, the world is purified, because judgment is great enlightenment as well as great burning. Under judgment sin is withered in us.

With the enlightenment from God, man can no longer live in sin. Error is not corrected by argument but by judgment. Once the light of judgment shines everything is known. Ever since the garden of Eden, judgment has always destroyed sin, for its light consumes. One day all the world's sins will be destroyed. The last destruction of sin will occur at the judgment of the great white throne. Without question, judgment has tremendous power.

When we look at judgment we are compelled to recognize who God is. To know God as Father is one thing; to know Him as God is quite another. Through redemption we know the Father; through judgment we know God and worship Him. Sin seems to have compromised the glory of God. Who achieves the upper hand on the earth—the righteous or the unrighteous, the crooked or the honest? Today people may have many reasons to misunderstand God, but one day He will manifest His glory. For God is holy, righteous and terrible. Through judgment He will be recognized as God. Then men will know the terror of the Lord. "Knowing therefore the terror of the Lord," wrote Paul, "we persuade men" (2 Cor. 5.11 Darby). Today the terror of the Lord may be only a teaching to many, but one day the whole world will receive this great revelation. God will not permit sin to continue any further.

Yet we need not wait till that day to know this. There will indeed be burning before the judgment seat of Christ when all that can be burned shall be consumed. The lake of fire will indeed follow the judgment of the great white throne. But we can learn to let that light of judgment enlighten us *today*. Let the light be as bright today as it will be in that day. Let it shine more than once till we are smitten (how useless are mental knowledge and mere teaching here). May God have mercy upon us if we are *in*creased instead of being *de*creased. May He be merciful to us if we are not yet consumed.

Here we are not simply preaching words. We want people to receive something vital that they may know what kind of persons they truly are before God. Let us truly understand that enlightening produces burning. And this fire shall burn forever. And this eternal fire shall guarantee the eternal newness of the new earth. This is the great gospel of salvation for the new earth. The power of sin is now forever under God's judgment.

This reality is seen in the City of God. Why is this city a city of gold? Because it is a city that has passed through the fire. Gold and precious stones have gone through the fire successfully. In essence, the New Jerusalem is fireproof. Many things in the old garden of Eden were consumed, but all in the City of the New Covenant shall endure the fire. Eternal fire thus guarantees the eternal purity of the world. God will not be misunderstood anymore, for there is power in judgment. God is light; let us therefore walk in the light and not in darkness. Amen!

3 | Judgment unto Victory

A bruised reed shall he not break, and smoking flax shall he not quench, till he send forth judgment unto victory. (Matt. 12.20)

Now from the sixth hour there was darkness over all the land until the ninth hour. And about the ninth hour Jesus cried with a loud voice, saying, Eli, Eli, lama sabach-thani? that is, My God, my God, why hast thou forsaken me? And some of them that stood there, when they heard it, said, This man calleth Elijah. And straightway one of them ran, and took a sponge, and filled it with vinegar, and put it on a reed, and gave him to drink. And the rest said, Let be; let us see whether Elijah cometh to save him. And Jesus cried again with a loud voice, and yielded up his spirit. And behold, the veil of the temple was rent in two from the top to the bottom; and the earth did quake; and the rocks were rent; and the tombs were opened; and many bodies of the saints that had fallen asleep were raised. (Matt. 27.45–52)

Whom [Christ] God set forth to be a propitiation,

through faith, in his blood, to show his righteousness because of the passing over of the sins done aforetime, in the forbearance of God; for the showing, I say, of his righteousness at this present season: that he might himself be just, and the justifier of him that hath faith in Jesus. (Rom. 3.25,26)

Now is the judgment of this world: now shall the prince of this world be cast out. (John 12.31)

And he, when he is come, will convict the world in respect of sin, and of righteousness, and of judgment: . . . of judgment, because the prince of this world hath been judged. (John 16.8,11)

What the law could not do, in that it was weak through the flesh, God, sending his own Son in the likeness of sinful flesh and for sin, condemned sin in the flesh. (Rom. 8.3)

God uses judgment to save the world. Judgment has power. It can consume as well as enlighten. Since the time of creation, there has been judgment after judgment that sin might be restricted, destroyed and stopped. At the end, there will be the judgments of the sheep and the goats, of the dragon, and of the great white throne. Because of these judgments, sin shall not be able to continue on anymore. Today sin appears to be victorious, but one day sin will be done away. Judgment is God's work in accomplishing His plan and purpose. So that it is not only terrible but also loving.

However, though it is useful to this earth, to the kingdom, to the new heaven and the new earth, and to the plan of God, it nevertheless contains no individual salvation. Hence, before the arrival of the last judgment, God sets up the cross, since in the cross there is found personal salvation. The cross saves not because it avoids judgment, for it would not be right to eliminate sin without judgment. No, the salvation of the cross does not set aside judgment; on the contrary, the cross saves because it is itself a judgment. What differs is that in the cross there is salvation but in the future judgment men shall be eternally condemned and bereft of salvation. So salvation does not overturn judgment; it actually fulfills judgment. Salvation is reached through judgment.

Therefore the cross is itself a judgment. Its enlightenment is not in any way less powerful than the enlightening of judgment. It is not behind judgment either in consuming sin or in glorifying God. Its power and work are as strong as those of the future judgment. When sin comes in, God uses judgment to solve it. Anything less than judgment cannot resolve the problem of sin. For this reason, the cross has the same intensity in its dealing with sin as the future judgment has. In the hearts of God's children the cross is living today. Let us now see how much our Lord has gone through for us.

In the early morning the Lord Jesus was led away to be judged by Pilate. He was crucified in the morning at about nine o'clock, and He died around three in the afternoon. One thing worth noticing: from the time the Lord was crucified until noon, nothing special happened. He prayed for the forgiveness of people's sin. Many think He was crucified by the wicked; and the book of Acts states: "ye by the hand of lawless men did crucify and slay" (Acts 2.23). Yet after the noon time, Jesus cried out, "My God, my God, why hast thou forsaken me?" (Matt. 27.46) Perhaps there has never been seen such weakness among the martyrs (the Lord forgive me for saying this). It would seem that the later Christian martyrs exhibited far more courage since none of them has ever said that God had forsaken him or her. On the contrary, all have praised and thanked God. Some were burned to death. Even with their bodies half-burned, they still praised God. At the moment they laid down their lives, they were found praising Him.

Why, then, did our Lord cry out, God has forsaken Me? For God *had* actually forsaken Him. The earthquake, the split rocks, the darkness—all showed that God's judgment was upon His Son in order that you and I might be freed. The cross, to our Lord, was judgment, given to Him by God. Death came upon Him, and even His Father left Him. Yet God's deliverance manifests His righteousness.

Justification by faith is cited in the book of Romans to show that God is just and righteous. Judgment proves how clear is God's righteousness. For righteousness is seen in judgment. We are saved because God has dealt with our sins. He does not overlook them. We are forgiven because God in Christ has paid it all. His forgiving us is wholly righteous. The cross will not be effective if its judgment is less intense than the future judgment. "For what the law could not do, in that it was weak through the flesh, God, sending his own Son in the likeness of sinful flesh and for sin, condemned sin in the flesh: that the ordinance of the law might be fulfilled in us" (Rom. 8.3,4). This is not only judgment but also condemnation. God has condemned sin in the flesh of our Lord in order that we might be delivered from the power of sin.

So that by the cross God has condemned sin to death through Christ Jesus. Through this light sin is condemned and consumed. This is the second thing which the Lord has done. For He was judged not only for sinners but also for sin. God has made Him who is sinless to be sin for us, and in His death sin died in Him forever. Thus the Lord said, ". . . of judgment, because the prince of this world hath been judged" (John 16.11).

The prince of this world is judged. How marvelous that in the death of our Lord the world was judged in its prince. Actually the cross was Satan's great gamble. He threw his all at the cross. There he gathered all the forces of nations, kings, people, and even death. He tried to put an end to Jesus' work once and forever. But our Lord arose from the dead and finished the devil off instead. Thus was the prince of this world judged. Hereafter all who have eternal life will declare that the satanic world is defeated. The hour the Lord's *heel* was crushed, Satan's *head* was crushed.

Hence the cross solves the problem of sins, and the power of sin, Satan and his world. The judgment of the cross today is just as powerful as the judgment of the future day. It has tremendous strength of burning as well as of enlightening.

In accepting the cross, it is not enough simply to accept God's love or forgiveness. The cross also stands for suffering, but it is not enough merely to accept it as suffering. The cross additionally means laying aside self and submitting to God, but still it is not enough to only accept it as that. No, the cross is equally a judgment by which God's aim is reached. It severely judges the sinners, the world, and the devil. Knowing the terror of the Lord we persuade men.

God does not expect His children to have their problems solved at the future judgment; He wants these resolved at the cross. For the people of the world, there remains a judgment wherein there is no salvation; but for God's children nothing should wait to be solved at the judgment seat of Christ, because God wants us to have everything cleared up at the cross. Therefore, our understanding of judgment must reach the depth of judgment.

Let us be reminded that all the sacrifices in the Old Testament represent the cross. And there was no sacrifice without fire. Without the fire there would be no acceptance by God. We are accepted through the burning of the sacrifice. Yet how we long for something to be left, but God will destroy everything till there is nothing more to be destroyed. We know that ash is the very last form of things. The cross will reduce a thing until God's fire can no longer reduce it any further. Then it can be used.

Judgment will bring you to a point where nothing in you can resist God. Under His judgment, everything is withered and weakened. The cross is an experience whereby you must once be so enlightened by God that you are reduced to ashes. There must be a time when your self-confidence and pride are brought to an end. Then will there be resurrection out of the ashes.

Yet once having suffered, how will you know that

the cross has done its work? You will know because
under God's intense light you lose your natural strength.
There is no man who can ever survive God's light; for
His enlightening is also a burning. As God shines, you
are consumed by fire. His judgment exposes all and also
burns all. Whenever God speaks, you are finished. But
if perchance you still live, you have merely heard doc-
trine. No one after he is enlightened is able to stir
himself up to do what he had done before. The problem lies in your starting to work after you have heard
the message, but you will find yourself unable to do
it again since that is not the work of God. Just as at
God's last judgment men will have no need to exert
themselves to deal with sin, so this should be true today. The light of judgment is able to break what you
were unable to overcome for many years. The cross
ought to be a judgment in your life which continually
delivers you from the world.

4 | Loving-kindness and Judgment

I will sing of loving-kindness and judgment: unto thee, Jehovah, will I sing psalms. (Ps. 101.1 Darby)

Therefore will Jehovah wait, that he may be gracious unto you; and therefore will he be exalted, that he may have mercy upon you: for Jehovah is a God of justice [or, judgment]; blessed are all they that wait for him. (Is. 30.18)

I can of myself do nothing: as I hear, I judge: and my judgment is righteous; because I seek not mine own will, but the will of him that sent me. (John 5.30)

As often as ye eat this bread, and drink the cup, ye proclaim the Lord's death till he come. Wherefore whosoever shall eat the bread or drink the cup of the Lord in an unworthy manner, shall be guilty of the body and the blood of the Lord. But let a man prove himself, and so let him eat of the bread, and drink of the cup. For he that eateth and drinketh, eateth and drinketh judgment unto himself, if he discern not the body. (1 Cor. 11.26–29)

But when we are judged, we are chastened of the Lord, that we may not be condemned with the world. (1 Cor. 11.32)

The cross of Christ reveals the attitude of God toward sin. In dealing with the Lord Jesus, God deals with sin because our Lord was made sin for us. All that is contrary to God must be completely destroyed. Forgiving is grace, whereas hating is judgment. God cannot cheaply forgive, since He so greatly hates sin. Salvation must correspond with His holiness. Toward sin, the cross is God's judgment; towards us, it is His forgiveness. We receive grace on the one hand and are judged on the other hand. We are a people judged as well as favored.

In 1 Corinthians 11, the word "unworthy" points to attitude, not to qualification. For there is none who is qualified. The body and the blood of the Lord are equivalent to the cross. Some people at the Lord's table, while eating and drinking, agree with the cross; but some do not agree. The issue is not whether they are good or bad before God, since no one is good; rather, it is their attitude toward sin. This determines who is in agreement and who is not. Hence let us judge ourselves, discerning the body of the Lord. Know what the Bread of God did for us. This is the judgment of the cross. For this bread on the table tells us that God does not allow anything to exist which is contradictory to himself. Hence we must judge ourselves. We are unworthy if we do not judge ourselves. The cross judges sin, the flesh, and the natural life. God judges everything opposing Him; do we judge the same? It is not a matter of whether or not we are good, for none of us is good. It is a matter of how we judge our "no good." People can even glory and boast in their "no good." We may say with pride that we are weak.

So the question is, God has already manifested His thought on the cross, but what about our attitude? In breaking the bread, the question to be asked is this: what attitude do God's children take towards the cross of Christ? This is not an exercise to try to make ourselves better or more presentable. For the knowledge of good and evil ends at the cross. It simply asks how we should look at ourselves. Under judgment we have nothing to say, nor will we compare ourselves with others. We stand on the ground of our being nothing good in order to come and break the bread. We thank God for His salvation on the one hand and we fear God for His judgment on the other hand.

How should we judge ourselves? Even man's repentance and confession of sin can easily come from himself, and not from God. Is this a matter of conduct or is this a matter of judgment? What is repentance as a result of judgment? At least we are saved; at least God has judged our many sins. At the time I was saved, for example, I was aware of my sins. But as I knelt to pray, God showed me within one or two minutes all my sins. What I saw within these minutes was different from what I saw before. Formerly I was indeed conscious of having sinned; but in these two minutes I felt so terribly sinful that I could not lift up my head. So I confessed my sins and asked God to forgive me.

When God executes judgment by enlightening you, you will fall under the light. After your sin is judged by the light, that particular sin can never raise its head again. It is instead destroyed. The light that causes a person to judge his own sin is the light of judgment.

No one can pass through God's light and live. For example, you cannot get rid of lying; but as the light of God shines, lying is eliminated. This is the work of God. It is the Lord who delivers. Some know how strong their natural life is, but they can do nothing about it. They may try to be humble before men. Yet only the light of judgment can break the power of death. They know, but this may only be a teaching to them.

There is a vast difference between teaching and revelation. Teaching is something one must do after hearing; whereas revelation is a seeing the thing as having already been done. When light comes, the problem is resolved. Great is the difference between our acknowledging sin by coming into some knowledge and our confessing sin under the light. Fierce and penetrating is the light of judgment. A sinner may live very comfortably, but when God's light strikes, he is finished and done for. Each person needs to have this basic enlightening which produces a lasting consequence. And when truly experienced, hereafter he will be able to judge himself.

The work of God was clearly manifested in Paul's conversion. This man hated the church and shed the blood of the saints. But while he was on the road to Damascus, the light of God shone upon him. He did not need to worry how he should deal with his hatred, because he had no such problem now; for when he rose up from the ground, he hated no more. Such is our salvation through judgment. What solves our insoluble problem is judgment. It is the cross. What man cannot do, God can.

How often a person has something he cannot overcome. He may make resolutions and shed many tears, but strangely all to no avail. Yet one day the light of judgment shines upon him, he is made to see the terribleness of that thing, and as he confesses his sin, that sin is taken away from him; for how can he now confess and still have that sin remain in him? During enlightenment, the power of sin is destroyed.

You may worry about your being no good, but actually you have never seen how weak and bad you truly are. You say you are weak because you have heard the teaching. God speaks, but you hear only teaching. As a result you pursue after holiness, you even admire it, yet you can do nothing about it. Accordingly, ask God to enlighten you with His strong light, and then what bothers you will be removed. God works through His light. Commit yourself, therefore, into His hand, and let His terrible light fall upon you. And if you allow yourself to be judged *today*, you will not be judged *later.*

Everybody must be enlightened and judged once. Even the unsaved will be judged one day. He who steals or murders will be caught one day by the law of the world; his suffering after being caught, however, will not even be one thousandth of the suffering in the future. But to be disciplined by the Lord is not the same as to be condemned by Him as are the people of the world. Actually, judgment is the Lord's mercy and grace to us. It is grace disguised in the form of the cross.

So let us sing of His loving-kindness and judgment! Let us sing the song of the Lamb and of Moses! (Rev. 15.3,4)

5 | Judgment in the House of God

For this cause many among you are weak and sickly, and not a few sleep. But if we discerned ourselves, we should not be judged. But when we are judged, we are chastened of the Lord, that we may not be condemned with the world. (1 Cor. 11.30-32)

The time is come for judgment to begin at the house of God: and if it begin first at us, what shall be the end of them that obey not the gospel of God? (1 Peter 4.17)

God is a righteous judge, yea, a God that hath indignation every day. (Ps. 7.11)

Jehovah will judge his people, and repent himself for his servants; when he seeth that their power is gone, and there is none remaining, shut up or left at large. (Deut. 32.36)

He calleth to the heavens above, and to the earth, that he may judge his people. (Ps. 50.4)

I will judge you, O house of Israel, every one according to his ways, saith the Lord Jehovah. Return ye, and turn yourselves from all your transgressions; so iniquity shall not be your ruin. (Ez. 18.30)

Zion shall be redeemed with justice, and her converts with righteousness. (Is. 1.27)

Jehovah may judge His people (Ps. 50.4). Judgment shall begin at the house of God, says the Lord. Naturally this points to the future, since the future judgment touches many areas and is composed of many parts, with the great white throne being the last portion. The first portion is the judgment of God's house today. Such judgment among God's children is continuous. Upon people in general judgment can be incidental, but in relation to God's people it is a constant affair. The cross is for the children of God.

Only God's children have the privilege of enjoying God's continual judgment. Those who are not God's children do not have this privilege: "when we are judged, we are chastened of the Lord, that we may not be condemned with the world" (1 Cor. 11.32). That we be judged is really grace and enjoyment; and as a consequence, we may not be condemned. Once in a while God will indeed judge the world to prevent it from becoming too corrupted. The Genesis flood, for example, was but a prevention. But in the lives of God's children, judgment is for the purpose of their being spared from future judgment. One day God will totally destroy the power of sin, but today He has it accomplished first in His children.

God enlightens as well as sets on fire. Today God's

children do not lack power; they lack enlightenment. We may think it takes power to eliminate improper things. Yet who of us knows that that which takes away all which is opposed and contrary to God is *enlightenment* and not power? When God enlightens you and shows you the sinfulness of sin, that sin leaves you. It is withered and gone. For light brings in conviction, and more light generates the power to eliminate sin. Let us be willing to be enlightened of God. For when we are enlightened, sin cannot raise its head.

What, though, if we fail to see this light? Let us understand that the fire from God is for burning. If it does not burn away sin, then it will burn away the person. Light rejected will mean we incur chastening. Chastening is not God's second act, but it simply comes at the time when light is rejected. Discipline or chastening is a kind of judgment. He who accepts the judgment of light is saved, whereas he who rejects the light is disciplined. Chastening is God's judgment. It comes as the result of light being rejected. Not all unfortunate happenings are necessarily God's chastening, though many of them are.

How do we know if a particular chastening is a satanic attack or the Lord's discipline? All who fear God will hear what God has to say. Yet many of God's children fail to see the light. Many chastenings fall short of their purposes. Even after chastenings, they still do not see wherein there is crookedness and unrighteousness in their lives. Let us therefore ask for enlightenment, for this truly is a blessing. Seeing light today is the proof that God's judgment is in His house.

Is it not surprising that God will sometimes judge the world in order to prevent sin, but that His judgment in His house is unceasing? Let us notice that in the Old Testament days God's judgment was always upon His house. At Kadesh-barnea, the children of Israel were afraid of the giant Anaks in Canaan, though God's witnesses Caleb and Joshua said the enemy was to be their "food" (see Num. 13,14). The greater the difficulty, the better the food. (Oh, how many of God's children are weak because they have never gone through difficulty! Their problem lies in their "food.") God dealt with His own people back then much harder than He dealt with the outside people. All who were above twenty years of age were told they would not be allowed to enter Canaan; and forty years would have to pass before the new generation itself could go in. When the people heard *this*, then they decided to obey and to fight. Yet God was not with the people for He had already judged them.

How merciful God was towards the gentile people in Nineveh, yet He would not allow His children—the Israelites—to enter the Promised Land! The closer one is to God, the severer is His discipline. It almost appears as though the farther a person is from God the easier it is for that one. And today as in the ancient days God pays very close attention to His people.

Another example from the Old Testament was the case of Miriam, who sinned by speaking against Moses for his taking a Cushite as wife; and she was struck down with leprosy. Though she was a prophetess among God's people, she had to be shut outside the camp. (God would not act the same way in the world.) She must be put to shame seven days as though her own father had spat in her face.

Take the case of Korah and his band of 250 men, who accused Aaron and Moses of elevating themselves above the congregation of the Lord. They argued that they too could serve God. In doing so, they overturned the delegated authority set up by the Lord. God strongly warned the other people in the congregation to depart from the tents of Korah, Dathan, and Abiram, for the ground later split apart from under them and they were swallowed alive unto Hades. God dealt with them severely because this was His house and not the world. Authority came through resurrection, it was not something vested in the flesh. Whenever the authority of resurrection is rejected, there comes forth death.

In history no nation suffered destruction more times than did the nation of Israel, because that nation was God's house. He had chosen them to manifest His ways; so whenever there was sin among them there was His judgment. Being God's house, they went under when they departed from God, but they rose above when they kept near Him. Not so with the world. It would seem that when the people of the world want to draw nigh to God they are chastened, but when they are far away from Him they enjoy prosperity. Yet with His children, the closer they are to God the more discipline they receive.

Continuing with the Old Testament examples, we find that after the time of the Judges, the judgment which fell upon the life of David exceeded the judgments which befell the other kings. Even King Saul was not as disciplined and judged as was David. When

David sinned, what he did in secret would be repaid to him in the open. One child of his died, and two of his sons were lost.

When the ark of God was carried on a new oxcart, the oxen stumbled and Uzzah reached forth towards the ark and took hold of it to steady it. Even though Uzzah meant it well, God struck Uzzah to death.

The degree of nearness to God decides the heaviness of chastening. Because they were God's house the children of Israel were judged many times. These instances but demonstrate God's work outwardly. Consider the priests of Israel. They must bear the sin against the sanctuary; they must bear the sin of their office. God could be lenient towards the *people* of Israel, but He was strict with their *priests*. An Israelite might bring a bullock and offer it as a sacrifice five months after he had sinned, but the priests in the holy temple must offer a sacrifice every day. For the priest it was not a case of three times a year to offer up a sacrifice. If the priest did not continually offer it up, he would die instantly. God could let the ordinary people go, but He would not allow the priests to do so.

We Christians today are God's house, we are all the temple of the living God. Just as the Lord required of the children of Israel long ago, so He requires of us. Either the light burns away sin or we receive chastening. We are judged because we are the temple of God. It is not easy to be a Christian, because he cannot resign or escape. A Christian is one who is to disregard his own feeling. The life of God as well as the Spirit of God is in him. Other people may live carelessly, but you and I cannot so live. The least contradiction will make us uneasy. And such is vital Christianity. Light reproves, and God judges to the extent that some may be weak, and some may even die.

Let us be careful not to let any uneasiness be overlooked. We will be sorry if God should let us go free. For nothing is worse than a beliver being given up by God. To be chastened is to be as a son; not to be chastened is to be as an illegitimate child. If someone should never be chastened, I should be fearful for him. Chastening serves as God's warning. When light is rejected, pray that you may see.

6 | Keep the Judgments of God

Moses came and told the people all the words of Jehovah, and all the ordinances [or, judgments]: and all the people answered with one voice, and said, All the words which Jehovah hath spoken will we do. (Ex. 24.3)

Ye shall therefore keep my statutes, and mine ordinances [or, judgments]; which if a man do, he shall live in them: I am Jehovah. (Lev. 18.5)

It shall come to pass, because ye hearken to these ordinances, and keep and do them, that Jehovah thy God will keep with thee the covenant and the lovingkindness which he sware unto thy fathers. (Deut. 7.12)

The Rock, his work is perfect; for all his ways are justice [or, judgment]: a God of faithfulness and without iniquity, just and right is he. (Deut. 32.4)

They shall teach Jacob thine ordinances [or, judgments], and Israel thy law: they shall put incense before thee, and whole burnt-offering upon thine altar. (Deut. 33.10)

He provided the first part for himself, for there was

the lawgiver's portion reserved; and he came with the heads of the people; he executed the righteousness of Jehovah, and his ordinances with Israel. (Deut. 33.21)

Blessed are they that keep justice, and he that doeth righteousness at all times. (Ps. 106.3)

With my lips have I declared all the judgments of thy mouth. . . . My soul breaketh for longing after thy judgments at all times. . . . I have chosen the way of faithfulness; thy judgments have I set before me. . . . And take not the word of truth utterly out of my mouth; because I have hoped in thy judgments. . . . I remembered thy judgments of old, O Jehovah, and have comforted myself. . . . I have not departed from thy judgments; for it is thou that hast taught me. . . . I have sworn, and I will perform it, that I will keep thy righteous judgments. . . . Accept, I beseech thee, Jehovah, the voluntary-offerings of my mouth, and teach me thy judgments. . . . My flesh shuddereth for fear of thee; and I am afraid of thy judgments. . . . Many are thy tender mercies, O Jehovah; quicken me according to thy judgments. . . . The sum of thy word is truth, and every righteous judgment of thine is for ever. . . . Hear my voice according to thy loving-kindness: O Jehovah, quicken me according to thy judgment. . . . Let my soul live, and it shall praise thee; and let thy judgments help me. (Ps. 119.13,20,30,43,53,102,106,108,120,156,160, 149,175 Darby)

In a controversy they shall stand to judge; according to mine ordinances shall they judge it: and they shall keep my laws and my statutes in all my appointed feasts; and they shall hallow my sabbaths. (Ez. 44.24)

Therefore have I hewed them by the prophets; I have

slain them by the words of my mouth: and thy judgments
are as the light that goeth forth. (Hosea 6.5)

All his ordinances were before me; and as for his
statutes, I did not depart from them. (2 Sam. 22.23)

How does God use enlightenment to judge and to
expose all that is hidden?

Judgment is God's answer to death, for He uses it
to get rid of sin. The cross is redemption, but it is also
judgment. We should accept the cross. The house of
God is constantly under His light of judgment. There
is the altar in God's temple. The temple of God is able
to stand because all must pass through the altar (the
altar serves as a type of the judgment of the cross).
Judgment is manifested daily in God's house. No one
can live in His house without being judged. As long
as God's temple exists, there ought to be enlightening.
The purpose of God's enlightening judgment is to keep
His children in full harmony with His holiness.

I would like to mention still another aspect of judgment (the Hebrew word *mishpat* can be translated ordinance or judgment). It is the keeping of the judgments
of God. God has declared that we should keep His
judgments. If we know them, we should also keep them.

In China there are laws which can neither be
changed or be added to. These are the decisions of the
Supreme Court.* They become the law of the land.

*The reader should keep in mind that the author was speaking in
1942.—*Translator*

God's judgments are God's laws. As His laws express His high wills, so His judgments manifest His mind. Hence we must keep His judgments in the church as much as we keep His laws. Judgment reveals the mind of God concerning a particular matter. Though it may happen in another's life, nevertheless I too must keep it. The judgment of God, therefore, becomes our law.

God's judgment is God's great enlightening which causes us to know our fault, know the sinfulness of sin, and know ourselves. There is unity in God's enlightenment, judgment, and condemnation. Some say the experience of Kadesh-barnea is but an historical fact; there is no command, hence it has nothing to do with us. Yet God considers it to be a judgment—which we must learn to keep. God will do the same thing today because His attitude toward sin has not changed.

All the past judgments are our judgments. God's judgment upon Moses for striking the rock twice for water, for example, is nothing less than a judgment meant for us to keep. If the same incident were to happen today, God would do the very same thing. Likewise, both the incidents of Uzzah and that of Korah with his band of 250 people were matters of God's judgment. And God's judgments remain forever. Thus do we realize what is meant by keeping the judgments of God. What God did among His people in the past, He will do the same in the church today.

Ephesus had been judged long ago by God; even today, there is no church in Ephesus. God's judgment has not changed at all. Everyone must keep it. We need to keep not only the judgments found in the Bible but also God's judgments throughout the twenty centuries of church history.

I well remember how one brother had the habit of criticizing others severely. On one occasion a second brother had lost his son, and this critical brother said that the son *should* have died because God was punishing the father. On another occasion a sister had lost her son, and this same critic commented again that unless there were repentance more would die. In so doing he was actually asking for God's judgment. Because he had no light before God, he had no right to criticize. What criticisms he gave were always done "in cold blood." Interestingly enough, a month afterwards two of his own sons died. Having neither by reason of the Blood nor authority and yet being sharply critical of people, he was opening the door for God's judgment to fall upon him.

Once two of the students in Shangtung Christian Medical College were engaged. And this same brother again criticized. I told him not to interfere and asked him why he had such an attitude. He had no answer but only harbored an evil intention of breaking up their engagement. One day severe judgment again fell on him: he was excommunicated by the church. Hence, either God gives you authority or you claim the blood of Christ with fear and trembling. For the judgment of God is very living. The same measure which you use, it shall be measured to you again (see Luke 6.38b). For this reason, learn to fear God's judgment. I dare not do anything that will invite His judgment upon me. God's judgment is exacting. If He judges a certain matter to be sinful, He will judge that very matter in our life as being sinful.

By reading the Bible we can learn to know what judgment God will pronounce on us if we are wrong as we see it executed upon other people who were sinful. We often learn our lessons from what happened to other brethren. Thus shall we make great progress. The proud, however, are unable to learn from others nor will they want to truly see themselves.

Judgment is a fundamental enlightening. Once having been smitten with judgment, one will see immediately with the least light. He is able to discern the light of judgment in the lives of other believers and learn from it. His spiritual advance will doubtless be quite noticeable. "Quicken me according to thy judgments," said the psalmist (119.156 Darby). Only God's judgment can quicken us into life. For as He judges, it will cause me to live as well as to die.

To keep the judgment of God is not something that just any person can do. It requires the experience of a fundamental enlightening in the person. Do not substitute the fragmentary for the fundamental, because fragmentary dealings will only increase a person's pride. The most difficult people to deal with are those with partial dealings. These partial dealings stand in the way of the large ones. Many fail in this area. May God so put us under His light that we cannot be our former selves anymore.

Saul of Tarsus fell to the earth as he was struck down by the light from heaven. He was never the same again. Such was God's judgment. When Saul rose up from the earth, he had to be led. He was helpless. Yet this is a most necessary work.

According to Genesis 1.1–2, the former world came under judgment. Light came in on the first day of restoration (God's works are all positive). The light on the first day, however, revealed the past judgment, for the earth was waste and empty, and darkness was upon the face of the deep. This judgment disclosed the true situation in the old creation. Judgment is executed on the past, not on the future. The sin of the world has already been judged. God does not give new judgment. He enlightens us concerning the past judgment. He shows us how He destroyed the old creation. He, of course, already had the knowledge, but we ourselves do not know. So one day we receive His enlightenment and begin to know the actual situation. Such is the fundamental and necessary work of God.

Therefore, the judgments and commands of the Lord must be kept. We must accept His judgments: first the fundamental, and then the fragmentary.

7 | Judge Them Who Are Within

And if thy brother sin against thee, go, show him his fault between thee and him alone: if he hear thee, thou hast gained thy brother. But if he hear thee not, take with thee one or two more, that at the mouth of two witnesses or three every word may be established. And if he refuse to hear them, tell it unto the church: and if he refuse to hear the church also, let him be unto thee as the Gentile and the publican. Verily I say unto you, What things soever ye shall bind on earth shall be bound in heaven; and what things soever ye shall loose on earth shall be loosed in heaven. (Matt. 18.15–18)

When he had said this, he breathed on them, and saith unto them, Receive ye the Holy Spirit: whose soever sins ye forgive, they are forgiven unto them; whose soever sins ye retain, they are retained. (John 20.22,23)

But Peter said, Ananias, why hath Satan filled thy heart to lie to the Holy Spirit, and to keep back part of the price of the land? While it remained, did it not remain thine own? and after it was sold, was it not in thy power? How is it that thou hast conceived this thing in thy heart? thou hast not lied unto men, but unto God. And Ananias hearing these words fell down and gave up the ghost: and great fear came upon all that heard it. And the young men arose and wrapped him round, and they carried him out and buried him. And it was about the space of three hours after, when his wife, not knowing what was done, came in. And Peter answered unto her, Tell me whether ye sold the land for so much. And she said, Yea, for so much. But Peter said unto her, How is it that ye have agreed together to try the Spirit of the Lord? behold, the feet of them that have buried thy husband are at the door, and they shall carry thee out. And she fell down immediately at his feet, and gave up the ghost: and the young men came in and found her dead, and they carried her out and buried her by her husband. (Acts 5.3–10)

It is actually reported that there is fornication among you, and such fornication as is not even among the Gentiles, that one of you hath his father's wife. And ye are puffed up, and did not rather mourn, that he that had done this deed might be taken away from among you. For I verily, being absent in body but present in spirit, have already as though I were present judged him that hath so wrought this thing, in the name of our Lord Jesus, ye being gathered together, and my spirit, with the power of our Lord Jesus, to deliver such a one unto Satan for the destruction of the flesh, that the spirit may be saved in the day of the Lord Jesus. Your glorying is not good. Know ye not that a little leaven leaveneth the whole lump? (1 Cor. 5.1–6)

What have I to do with judging them that are without?
Do not ye judge them that are within? (1 Cor. 5.12)

Today the house of the Lord is the sphere of God's judgment. He judges through His church. He not only judges in the church but also judges through the church. In the outer court the light is natural; in the holy place it is artificial, man-made light; but in the holiest of all there is neither natural nor artificial light; there is only the light of the glory of God. Only in the holiest of all will you see God's light. Consequently, the condemnation in the holiest is more severe than in any other place. If there is sin, it needs to be exposed to the light of the holiest.

Formerly the tabernacle was inanimate material, now it is living. God's light is in the sanctuary. The church today is the sanctuary where God's light is manifested. Though many times God will enlighten directly, many more times He will enlighten through the church. God gives light to men through the church. Hence judgment is not only in *God's* hand, it is also in the hand of the *church*.

In 1 Corinthians 5 it is said that we do not judge those outside but we do judge those who are within the church. The light in the sanctuary is to enlighten the sanctuary. So God's light will shine and judge when people in the church fail to see. The posture of 1 Corinthians 5 is not a sitting on the legal bench judging those who are beneath. It is rather the expression of the mourning of the church. For in the church there is no judge yet there is judgment. The judgment of the church is therefore neither positional nor authoritative. It ought instead to be that which brings forth repentance and sorrow.

The sinner in question in 1 Corinthians 5 had not been excommunicated, and the church had grown boastful and was without any sorrow. Yet the judgment of the church should result in humility and mourning. Had there been the light of judgment present, the church in Corinth would have prostrated herself before God for the sin in her midst and risen up to cast out the sin. The church cannot judge until light shines in her. She is not to be authoritative but mournful. She must judge herself first; she herself must repent, and *then* exercise discipline. Otherwise, excommunication becomes something legalistic.

In Matthew 18 we are told about one brother who had sinned against another brother. Now if he did not listen to the church, he would have to be treated as one of the gentiles. God honors the church where His light resides. Whatever is done on earth is also done in heaven. Let us therefore be careful not to speak against the church. In this world there are only natural light and artificial light; only in the sanctuary of God is there divine light. If there be no light in the sanctuary, there will be no light of God in the world. But the Lord does not forsake His church. So that His church has not changed; instead, her spiritual reality remains. For this reason, the Lord dared to say that if one will not listen to the church, let him be looked upon as one of the unbelievers. Our Lord dares to say, and I dare to believe.

The Lord Jesus is able to entrust judgment into the

hands of the church, because He believes in the work
of the Holy Spirit on earth. On the sixth day of creation, God breathed into the earthen body of man and
made him a living soul. After His resurrection, Jesus
said to His disciples, Receive ye the Holy Spirit (and
this word is spoken to the whole church). On the day
of resurrection, after the Holy Spirit is breathed in, the
church becomes alive and is able to judge. The church
is now the judgment of God. Interestingly, the Prot-
estants are afraid to use this word, while the Catholics
exploit this word; but we ourselves must look for
spiritual reality. According to the Bible, judgment *is* in
the church, for in God's word we find that there are
reproaches in the church, and even excommunication.
Ordinarily there will be confrontation, such as when
Paul confronted Peter. All these actions are for the sake
of restoration. But after every measure is exhausted,
the last measure used is judgment. Yet if today's judgment cannot restore, then the restoration must wait until
the time of future judgment; nevertheless, the spirit of
that person will still be saved.

All the truths in the Bible have subjective values.
Without light the church can neither speak nor judge.
Oftentimes you know a brother is wrong—is very wrong
indeed; yet you do not have the word to speak against
it. You sense the wrong quite deeply inside yourself, yet
you cannot utter it strongly outside. This is due to the
insufficiency of the inner light. Consequently, you are
unable to deal with that sin. Without the necessary
word, your persuasion would be ineffective. No word
because of insufficient light can only result in insufficient judgment. Day after day you notice his wrong,

until one day you are truly angry at the thing which is so contradictory to God (man can become irritated, but he does not know how to be angry). As you become angry, you know what to say to him for you have at last touched the root of the matter. With the result that judgment begins in the house of God. You are now able to persuade him, even to reprove him.

Let us understand that all the judgments of God are related to the anger of God. Yet God never loses His temper. Such anger is the strength of His judgment. Love is God's positive strength; patience is God's waiting strength; whereas anger is His destroying strength. Anger destroys all that is contrary to God. So far as the Lord is concerned, His love, patience and anger are tremendously great. When God becomes angry, sin is destroyed. So is it with the judgment of the church. As long as *God* forbears a matter, you have absolutely no way to rightly judge that matter. Only at the moment when God's light comes and exposes its wickedness will you have the anger of God placed in you (but without losing your temper). Then you can invite your brother to come and be reproved of you.

It is more difficult to reprove than to comfort. Love is what you should show daily; but anger is rather unusual. When you first perceive the wickedness of sin, you have no strength to judge. Only as light shines does the anger of God become your strength to judge. A weak person may scold but cannot reprove. To reprove and to scold are quite different actions. Losing one's temper is a losing of one's self-control; but anger is what God has added in. In anger there should be the power of self-control. In the case of Peter and Ananias, Peter did not lose his temper while talking severely with Ananias. His words were most rational. This was the anger of judgment. The first step in any judgment of the church is to reprove; the last step is to excommunicate.

When God's judgment is executed in the church, then besides repentance there will be one of two other consequences: (1) all communications are interrupted; the person will be looked upon as one of the gentiles; he cannot pray or have his prayer answered. (2) there may be physical punishment. The light of judgment in the church is serious. If it does not result in (1), it will end up with (2). Either there will be no communication or there will be death. Both are very serious. All who live before God should avoid such consequences.

Judgment is the greatest trial for many children of God to experience. Unless there is the fear of the Lord, how can one praise Him under judgment? Suppose your closest relative is going to hell, what will you say about it? Abraham was a good brother in the Lord, but he had to see Ishmael go. We may not be able to do that. In the case of both Ishmael and Isaac, Abraham did not look like a dear and loving father. For the believer, however, one thing is greater than affection, and that is the glory of God. This glory is to be our very life. When God's glory suffers, we must praise Him in judgment.

Why must the church judge? It is not because there may be a lack of brotherly love, but because of the need to maintain the glory of God. In the Old Testament days there were two great crises in the life of God's people: they came out of Egypt and they entered the Promised Land. In relation to these two crises, we see that God used judgment to maintain His glory. First, we learn how He judged the grave issue of the worship of idols. After Moses reproved the children of Israel for their sin surrounding the golden calf, he stood at the gate of the camp and asked who of them were on the Lord's side. And all the sons of Levi gathered to him. They were then ordered by Moses to go throughout the camp and slay their friends and relatives. For the sons of Levi it was a case of either upholding human affection or the glory of God. As a consequence of their allegiance to Him, God chose the Levites to serve Him forever.

According to men's thinking, it is not a good thing for brother to kill brother; but according to God's mind, it is deemed a very good thing, because such drastic action was taken for the purpose of restoring the damaged glory of God. The basic condition for ministry is to disregard human feeling out of a higher concern for the glory of God. In the case of Ai, Achan sinned and came short of the glory of God. Things that were ordered to be devoted exclusively to the Lord must be burned or destroyed before the Lord. But Achan did not offer up the devoted things for burning. So God desired His people to judge this sin by stoning Achan to death. Although God did not execute His judgment directly, He did do so indirectly. God will not spare your feeling. Either human feeling is given top priority or else the glory of God is.

The evidence that the glory of God was maintained during the Exodus period can be seen in what the Levites did; and the evidence that God's glory was preserved after the Israelites entered Canaan is demonstrated by the way God's people dealt with Achan. God entrusts the church with the responsibility of preserving His glory. The ultimate judgment of excommunication is something rare; being dealt with by the light of judgment is much more common. When God gives you the strength of anger, the consequence will be either deliverance or spiritual death. The church gives light to save or else there will be no more light if previous light is rejected.

In conclusion, then, during these seven days together we have been occupied with the subject of the Spirit of Judgment. First of all, we learned that God uses judgment to maintain His glory and to eradicate sin and whatever else is contrary to Him. Second, judgment to us is light. God's judgments are known in the words of His prophets. Third, the cross is but a moving the future judgment up to today. The cross is not an escaping of judgment, for it is itself a judgment. Fourth, judgment is today in the house of God. When our Lord was on earth, He twice in His anger drove the cattle away from the temple and overturned the tables of the money changers. Although our Lord did not beat people, He did become angry in the temple (which is a type of the church). So judgment is in God's house, and you cannot escape it.

To sum up. The power of sin is destroyed. Under the enlightenment of God's judgment and the cross, you (1) come to know yourself and (2) are chastened. The worst thing one can do is to take scourging as something incidental. Yet God is able to work out His salvation if you and I know the light of scourging. God's light will follow the scourge. Our God is to be feared. Through the reproof and judgment of the ministers in the church, you are made to see light or are made to suffer chastening physically, in order that day by day you may be more like Christ and glorify Him increasingly.

May the Lord grant to all of us the fundamental judgment so that we may daily keep the judgments of God.

PART TWO

THREE BASIC LESSONS*

*See *Translator's Preface* to this volume for background information
concerning these Lessons and their inclusion here.

1 | The Kingdom*

According to prophecies recorded in the Bible, the condition of the kingdom or nation will become increasingly serious. For nation shall rise against nation, and kingdom against kingdom. The structure of the government will become tighter and tighter. And as the book of Revelation predicts, it will be found that with the manifestation of the Antichrist, "no man [shall] be able to buy or to sell, save he that hath the mark, even the name of the beast or the number of his name" (13.17). This too will constitute a most serious affair. Hence we need to talk somewhat concerning the matter of the kingdom or nation.

(1) God Has Called Us to Enter the Kingdom of His Son

Whatever the Lord fared while on earth, that is what

---

*A message given by the author in 1948 at the Mount Kuling Conference Center near Foochow, China.

we too will fare on earth. And whatever He will have on earth in the future, we shall also share with Him. The psalmist declares: "Jehovah saith unto my Lord, Sit thou at my right hand, until I make thine enemies thy footstool" (Ps. 110.1). The Lord Jesus is now waiting for God to give Him the kingdoms of the world to be His footstool. He is above all politics. He is to set up another kingdom, even the kingdom of the heavens. All who are called out of the nations and kingdoms of this world are destined to be the citizens of His kingdom to come. We believers have a share in that kingdom because of the life which God has given to us. This is the Christian's position towards that kingdom.

The course which God has chosen for Christ is our course too. Just as the Lord does not assume management over any kingdom today, so this is to be our attitude as well. One day He shall rule the nations with an iron rod; thus will His kingdom come. And at that time we too shall have our kingdom.

The Lord tells us to bless the nations, not to curse them (1 Tim. 2.1–4). Only at the opening of the fifth seal (as recorded in Revelation) will the souls underneath the altar ask for vengeance and not for blessing. When the Lord was asked to divide the inheritance for some people, His answer was: "Man, who made me a judge or a divider over you?" (Luke 12.14) That was a civil case, it was not what a Christian today should do. On another occasion, when a woman taken in adultery was brought to the Lord, instead of her being condemned by the Lord, she was set free with these words: "Neither do I condemn thee: go thy way; from henceforth sin no more" (John 8.11b). This was a criminal case, and our Lord would not lift up His hand at all; rather, He wrote on the ground with His finger and let the dust be blown away. That was the Lord's way for handling the situation, and it is to be as well the way for us who have fellowship with Him. "I think," said Paul, that "God hath set forth us the apostles last of all, as men doomed to death" (1 Cor. 4.9a). It would therefore be highly abnormal for the Corinthian or any other believers to reign today in this world (cf. v.8).

(2) Concerning Political Problems

What I have reference to here concerns the matter of entering into politics, of being an official whether of high or low rank, of participating in the politics of the country. God's children often observe: "Who is worthy to govern this world? It would seem to be that only when Christians govern a nation's affairs is it really helpful to the people." Of course, it would be good if Christians were to manage a nation's affairs. But what, according to the Bible, is the Christian's way? Has not our Lord distinctly said: "My kingdom is not of this world: if my kingdom were of this world, then would my servants fight" (John 18.36a)? The nations on earth are now under the power of Satan, but we who know the Lord have been transferred into the kingdom of the Son of God's love (Col. 1.13). Our citizenship is in heaven (Phil. 3.20a).

In Rome there were people without the public rights of citizenship. On earth we are but strangers and sojourners, as Peter once said (cf. 1 Peter 2.11); hence we have no public rights on earth. But we do have the public rights of citizenship in heaven. Down here we are but law-abiding people, but up above is where our public rights are. Christians of whatever nationality are being delivered out of the kingdom of the world and are becoming heavenly citizens. On earth we are aliens, for the New Testament Greek word for "strangers" may also be translated as "aliens." The command of the Lord is: "All authority hath been given unto me in heaven and on earth. Go ye therefore, and make disciples of all the nations" (Matt. 28.18,19a). This clearly indicates that in one sense we are not in the world; otherwise there would be no need for us to be told to go. We are heavenly citizens touching the world with the gospel. For this reason we say that believers on earth must indeed be law-abiding, but that they are not to view themselves as citizens having public rights in the kingdom of the world. Stephen testified how the people of Israel had been sojourners and strangers in Egypt (Acts 7.6) and how Moses had become a sojourner in the land of Midian (Acts 7.29). Now being aliens and strangers like them because of our citizenship in heaven, we therefore hesitate to lay claim to earthly public rights since the claims of our heavenly citizenship take priority over them.

A few more words need to be added with respect to this matter of citizenship. Paul did indeed use the so-called rights of Roman citizenship three times as recorded in the book of Acts, but these rights he used only because of injustice having been meted out upon him in the given circumstance. In chapter 16, we find that Paul would not consent to his being punished uncondemned; in chapter 22 verses 24ff. we see he would not allow himself to be examined by scourging; and in chapter 25, we find he would finally appeal to Caesar. In each of these instances, Paul reluctantly claimed his rights of Roman citizenship in order to compel the governing authorities to uphold the law in a just manner.

(3) Concerning Public Offices

How can a Christian be an authority on earth before he is rewarded by the Lord with the authority to rule over certain numbers of cities (see Luke 19.16ff.)? Let us see that in regards to Christian reaction to ill-treatment, we believers have been instructed that we may not appeal to the courts (see 1 Cor. 6.1–8). How, then, can we be judges if we are not even supposed to be plaintiffs?

Why can we not be judges? Because this is the age of grace and God wants us to love people. Yet if one is to be a good official, he must be righteous. To maintain justice interferes with love; not to maintain justice violates the principle of righteousness. It is therefore impossible to preserve the characteristic of a Christian by assuming public office. The ministry of justice is required of a public servant, whereas the ministry of love and grace is demanded of a Christian.

It is quite true that Daniel, Esther, Mordecai, and others were in public office; but they were all captives without any choice in the matter. They were used of God after the nation of Israel had been judged and taken into captivity. Now if they had *sought* or *aspired* to serve in these capacities, that would have been a despicable act. Yet because they were captives, they were required to submit to human authorities and become public officials.

The Bible does teach us to be in subjection to the higher powers (see Rom. 13.1), but nowhere in the Scriptures are we instructed to assume earthly public office. Hence to become a government official is a decision made according to one's own thought. There is no command in the word of God. The Bible teaches us how to be masters and servants, but it has no teaching on how to be public officials.

(4) Concerning the Believer's Attitude towards Politics

"Let every soul be in subjection to the higher powers: for there is no power but of God; and the powers that be are ordained of God" (Rom. 13.1). God has set on earth two institutions: one is the state or kingdom, the other is the church. The government has authority, but so does the church have authority. God is the source of all governmental powers. All the powers on earth are ordained of God for good. If these powers or authorities should rebel and resist Him, they will sooner or later be removed. They are all under the control of God's authority. Even a policeman is ordained of God. So that the Lord has commanded us to be in subjection, though He has not charged us to be powers in the world. We must be in subjection to all state authorities. And likewise in the church, we submit ourselves as well to all spiritual authorities there.

God so sets up powers on earth that Christians should have no reason to fear them. We believe in government; we reject anarchy. The powers which are ordained of God are done so in order to punish the evil and to approve the good (Rom. 13.3). And even though such powers may go wrong, the principles of punishing the evil and approving the good can never be wrong. Those who execute the law must themselves keep the law. Governing authorities dare not openly declare that they will punish the lawful.

For the sake of conscience, Christians should be in subjection to the government which God has set up on earth: "Render to all their dues: tribute to whom tribute is due; custom to whom custom; fear to whom fear; honor to whom honor" (Rom. 13.7). It is a Christian duty to learn to pay the tax. "Be subject," said Peter, "to every ordinance of man for the Lord's sake: whether to the king, as supreme; or unto governors, as sent by him for vengeance on evil-doers and for praise to them that do well" (1 Peter 2.13,14).

(5) Concerning the Limits of Obedience

God alone deserves unlimited obedience; all others who exceed the measure of authority which God has given are not worthy of obedience. The obedience which a Christian renders to his country is not absolute. Obedience is a matter of action, whereas submission is one of attitude. From the book of Exodus we learn that the Hebrew midwives did not do what Pharaoh of Egypt commanded them—to kill all male children born to Hebrew women; and neither did Moses' mother obey this same decree of Pharaoh. Because the command of Pharaoh was contradictory to the law of God, it need not and should not be obeyed. Again, Daniel's three friends disobeyed the king's order, and they were commended by God. Daniel himself refused to follow the king's decree and was thrown into the lions' den; he too was approved of God. When Herod ordered to be killed all the male children in Bethlehem and its borders from two years old and under, Joseph took the baby Jesus and departed into Egypt.

Unless the order of the country's authorities contradicts God's laws or commands, we should learn to obey such authorities. Yet Peter and John said to the ruling authorities of their day who had forbade them to speak or teach in the name of Jesus, "Whether it is right in the sight of God to hearken unto you rather than unto God, judge ye: for we cannot but speak the things which we saw and heard" (Acts 4.19,20). If any nation's ruling powers take the step of persecuting us for religious reasons, we need not obey, but should submit ourselves even to the extent of our being put in jail.

(6) Concerning Revolution

Submission is unconditional, whereas obedience is limited. For this reason, God will not allow any Christian to start a revolution. Not to obey is permissible, but to submit in attitude is obligatory. Insubmission is reckoned as rebellion.

Wherever we go, we should submit to the authority of the local government. If we resist, we will be resisting God. In the event we cannot stand the oppression, we may move away to another city; for let us realize that we are here to save people, not to overthrow them. To flee from one city to another is the Lord's command (Matt. 10.23a).

(7) Concerning War

In the Old Testament period we find that God is a God who goes to war. He is called "Jehovah of hosts." Many of the battles which Israel fought were ordained of God. In the future at Har-Magedon (see Rev. 16.14,16; also, Zech. 14.2), God will gather the nations to war. So we cannot say that war is totally unjustified. However, during this period of grace, the Lord Jesus announces to his followers: "Blessed are the peacemakers: for they shall be called sons of God" (Matt. 5.9). He also declares this: "My kingdom is not of this world" (John 18.36a). Hence He wants us to preach the gospel of grace to men during this period of time. His word to Peter was: "Put up the sword into the sheath" (John 18.11a). Now is the time to put up the sword into the sheath. If this matter of war is left to our choice, no Christian may approve of war nor engage in it; but if we are forced into it, we as Christians will not bear arms but will be prepared to suffer the consequences for not doing so. It is good for the Christian not to be forced upon with respect to carrying arms. May we ask God to deliver us from it. Though war is permitted to happen by God, we as Christians must not take part in it.

2 | The Second Coming of the Lord*

Ye come behind in no gift; waiting for the revelation of our Lord Jesus Christ. (1 Cor. 1.7)

They themselves report concerning us what manner of entering in we had unto you; and how ye turned unto God from idols, to serve a living and true God, and to wait for his Son from heaven, whom he raised from the dead, even Jesus, who delivereth us from the wrath to come. (1 Thess. 1.9,10)

Our citizenship is in heaven; whence also we wait for a Saviour, the Lord Jesus Christ. (Phil. 3.20)

The grace of God hath appeared, bringing salvation to all men, instructing us, to the intent that, denying ungodliness and worldly lusts, we should live soberly and righteously and godly in this present world; looking for

*A message given by the author in 1948 at the Mount Kuling Conference Center near Foochow, China. In accordance with the Scriptures, the principle laid down here is that, just as Christ at His first coming concentrates on solving *spiritual* problems and leaves

the blessed hope and appearing of the glory of the great God and our Saviour Jesus Christ. (Titus 2.11-13)

Let not your heart be troubled: believe in God, believe also in me. In my Father's house are many mansions; if it were not so, I would have told you; for I go to prepare a place for you. And if I go and prepare a place for you, I come again, and will receive you unto myself; that where I am, there ye may be also. (John 14.1-3)

As often as ye eat this bread, and drink the cup, ye proclaim the Lord's death till he come. (1 Cor. 11.26)

Ye men of Galilee, why stand ye looking into heaven? this Jesus, who was received up from you into heaven, shall so come in like manner as ye beheld him going into heaven. (Acts 1.11)

Christ also, having been once offered to bear the sins of many, shall appear a second time, apart from sin, to them that wait for him, unto salvation. (Heb. 9.28)

He who testifieth these things saith, Yea: I come quickly. Amen: come, Lord Jesus. (Rev. 22.20)

This last verse of the last chapter in the last book of the Bible was written about sixty years after the ascension of the Lord. The Holy Spirit has already come, and of the original twelve apostles only one was still alive. The Lord is coming soon.

---

the other problems such as the *social* or *political* ones to be resolved at His second coming, so our calling today as His followers is to come out of the world rather than to change the world. The author does not mean to imply, however, that Christians should do nothing to help alleviate the sufferings of the world, since Christ in His earthly days also healed the sick and fed the needy.—*Translator*

We must not only look back to the cross but also look forward to the Lord's return. The grace of God which has brought salvation to us is to enable us to wait for the glorious appearing of the Lord. We should therefore serve the living God on the one hand and wait for the Lord's return on the other. Though we yet live on this earth, we break bread to remember the Lord till He comes. Though we lay stress on service as to how we need to fulfill the priestly ministry, we nevertheless know that such service on earth will not continue forever. One day we shall become the bride of the Lamb. All the objectives of the believers are not earthly. However much we may emphasize the local church, even that will not last on earth. We are looking and waiting for the Lord's return. The calling of God for us is not earthly, but heavenly. In sum, God has not called us to build permanently on earth.

According to the signs of the times given in the Bible, the coming of the Lord is undoubtedly near. Let us therefore wait, which means that whatever we do is for the sake of awaiting His return. Miss Margaret E. Barber was one who awaited the coming of the Lord with a single mind. Nothing about her had any permanent note. "I may suddenly meet the Lord," she once said, "at the next turn."

Since ours is a heavenly calling, there is nothing permanent or timeless on earth. As soon as we come to the Lord, we become the people who wait for the Lord's return. We are waiting for His coming, and not simply knowing that He will return. Not all who study the book of Revelation necessarily wait for the Lord's coming. Some people are well acquainted with the great white throne, the new heaven and the new earth, and other prophecies, but they may not be waiting for the coming of the Lord.

We are not out to change the world; rather, we are called out to be those who are unto the Lord. We entertain no hope of this earth, nor do we anticipate anything from the world. At His first coming, the Lord delivers us from sin and grants us the life of God that we may commune with God. This, however, is only half of the work. Though the question of sin is solved, the problem of death yet remains. The dominion of sin in man's life is over, but the kingdom of Satan still lingers. The power of death is broken, nevertheless our mortal bodies may yet die. Although we are saved, we continue to live in this corrupt environment. The holier the life, the deeper the feeling over the defilement of this world. The salvation which we now experience is but half the story, because the Lord Jesus—though He has saved us—has not yet changed the world.

The World

The second coming of the Lord is to change the world. He will not only give us enjoyment within but also allow us to enjoy the environment without because He will change the environment on earth. Many people are interested in social problems. They argue: "The salvation of the Lord saves only individuals but leaves the world full of inequality. Even the lower animals suffer so much. All the things in the world serve as enticements to men to sin. Though individuals may be saved, what about all these negative social conditions?"

As to this matter of waiting for the Lord's second coming, there appear to be two different concepts held among Christians. On the one hand, some believers are set on improving the world, but unfortunately they end up being defiled by it instead. On the other hand, others say that our responsibility is to rescue people out, and that the improvement of this world must wait till the Lord's return.

The Bible is not lax with respect to these matters. God has not said that so long as sinners are saved and are assured of going to heaven that that is enough. The Bible entertains no such thought. For heaven is not a matter of individual salvation; there is also the matter of the new heaven and new earth, which comes when— and only when—all who are ordained to eternal life have believed in the Lord. The Bible does have the salvation of society or the salvation of the world in view, but this work will be completed only with the second coming of the Lord. Today the church is commissioned to preach the gospel that individuals within the world may be saved, and yet the Lord has not forgotten the world. We are called today to rescue people out of the world, and not to change the world itself. This world has absolutely no hope whatsoever. All the problems on earth will only be solved at the Lord's return.

Some Basic Problems

On the earth there are a number of basic problems: (1) *Injustice*—God has said that only when His Son comes again shall righteousness be manifested: "With righteousness shall he judge the poor, and decide with equity for the meek of the earth; and he shall smite the earth with the rod of his mouth; and with the breath of his lips shall he slay the wicked" (Is. 11.4).

(2) *War*—There has always been the slaughtering of mankind on this earth. What the world needs most is peace. At the coming of the Lord, war shall be put to an end: "He will judge between the nations, and will decide concerning many peoples; and they shall beat their swords into plowshares, and their spears into pruning-hooks; nation shall not lift up sword against nation, neither shall they learn war any more" (Is. 2.4). Peace comes from the Lord and from no one else.

(3) *Public Health*—We have no absolute control over pestilences. According to Jeremiah and Ezekiel, they are fully controlled only by God. At the return of our Lord, all these shall pass away: "the inhabitant shall not say, I am sick: the people that dwell therein shall be forgiven their iniquity" (Is. 33.24). People will also live long too: "There shall be no more thence an infant of days, nor an old man that hath not filled his days; for the child shall die a hundred years old, and the sinner being a hundred years old shall be accursed" (Is. 65.20).

(4) *Hunger*—This is a major problem. Farm produce does not meet the world's needs. The whole world looks most attentively at this problem. A strange phenomenon prevails on earth, which is, that farm produce is difficult to grow whereas weeds grow quite easily and quite profusely. It is the weeds which squeeze out the wheat, not the wheat the weeds. A little carelessness in pulling out the weeds may at the same time destroy the wheat and ultimately hurt the harvest (see Matt.

13.28-30). This confirms that the curse on earth as told of in Genesis 3.17b,18 is indeed a fact ("Cursed is the ground for thy sake; in toil shalt thou eat of it all the days of thy life; thorns also and thistles shall it bring forth to thee; and thou shalt eat the herb of the field").

The weeds seem to grow naturally, while the corn is difficult to grow even with the help of fertilizers. In order to obtain food, man has to improve farm produce. This indicates how much time and energy man must invest in order that he may have food. If he should simply rely on nature, he would have nothing to eat. Truly, therefore, in the sweat of his face shall he eat bread.

It awaits the return of the Lord to solve this problem completely: "Behold, I will do a new thing; now shall it spring forth; shall ye not know it? I will even make a way in the wilderness, and rivers in the desert. The beasts of the field shall honor me, the jackals and the ostriches; because I give waters in the wilderness, and rivers in the desert, to give drink to my people, my chosen" (Is. 43.19,20)—"The wilderness and the dry land shall be glad; and the desert shall rejoice, and blossom as the rose" (Is. 35.1)—"Jehovah hath comforted Zion; he hath comforted all her waste places, and hath made her wilderness like Eden, and her desert like the garden of Jehovah; joy and gladness shall be found therein, thanksgiving, and the voice of melody" (Is. 51.3).

Today the earth is under a curse, and thus it does not produce efficiently. It is obviously no longer a paradise, for in a paradise corn should be able to grow spontaneously. But at the return of the Lord, there will

be the times of the restoration of all things. All the fields
on earth will produce abundantly for man, and there
will be no more growth of thorns and weeds. Even
without the help of fertilizers, the earth shall yield
much.

(5) *Education* — This surely is a basic need for society. Man should be instructed to know good and evil.
But at the return of Christ, the knowledge of the Lord
shall fill the earth completely: "They shall not hurt nor
destroy in all my holy mountain; for the earth shall be
full of the knowledge of Jehovah, as the waters cover
the sea" (Is. 11.9) — "this is the covenant that I will make
with the house of Israel after those days, saith Jehovah;
I will put my law in their inward parts, and in their heart
will I write it; and I will be their God, and they shall
be my people. And they shall teach no more every man
his neighbor, and every man his brother, saying, Know
Jehovah; for they shall all know me, from the least of
them unto the greatest of them, saith Jehovah: for I
will forgive their iniquity, and their sin will I remember
no more" (Jer. 31.33-34).

(6) *Recreation and Amusement Places* — Sinful
recreation and amusement places such as bars, opium
dens, gambling casinos, theaters, prostitution houses,
and so forth provide conveniences for people to sin.
In every city and every village, there are places such as
these causing man to fall. All these shall be eliminated
at the coming of the Lord: "The Son of man shall send
forth his angels, and they shall gather out of his
kingdom all things that cause stumbling, and them that
do iniquity" (Matt. 13.41).

(7) *Cruelty to Animals* — If human life is considered

by the world as cheap and worthless, how much more worthless are the lives of animals considered to be. Even tigers and lions suffer at the hands of man. Though there are societies for the prevention of cruelty to animals, these lower animals will groan in bondage until they finally are emancipated at the Lord's return: "we know that the whole creation groaneth and travaileth in pain together until now" (Rom. 8.22) — "the wolf shall dwell with the lamb, and the leopard shall lie down with the kid; and the calf and the young lion and the fatling together; and a little child shall lead them. . . . And the sucking child shall play on the hole of the asp, and the weaned child shall put his hand on the adder's den. They shall not hurt nor destroy in all my holy mountain; for the earth shall be full of the knowledge of Jehovah, as the waters cover the sea" (Is. 11.6,8,9).

(8) *Politics*—The whole world, whether at the international or at the domestic level, is engaged in striving for political power. Yet at the coming of the Lord, the seventh angel shall sound the trumpet and great voices in heaven shall declare: "The kingdom of the world is become the kingdom of our Lord, and of his Christ: and he shall reign for ever and ever" (Rev. 11.15).

At His first coming, the Lord's gospel solves my personal problem of sin; but at His second coming, He shall solve all the problems on earth. What the Lord Jesus does today is mainly on a personal basis, not on institutional ground. It awaits His second coming for all the problems on earth to be solved by means of His government. Today we are men of unclean lips dwelling in the midst of a people of unclean lips (Is. 6.5); but in the future we shall be clean men standing among a clean people. It is absolutely impossible for man to establish love through hatred. Any human attempts to establish' peace and prosperity today are subject to human error and can possibly lead to indescribable sufferings of mankind as a consequence. But when the Lord shall come, all will be perfectly established. How siginificant indeed is the second coming of the Lord.

The Lord Is Coming

Our calling is heavenly, and it is not for the purpose of changing this piece of earth. Nothing is permanent with us, nothing is indispensable. According to the Lord's arrangement, it is equally good for us to have or not to have. Everything will be fine if He comes. We live for His sake, and we wait for His return. At His coming our salvation shall be completed. Not only I personally shall be changed, even the environment shall be changed. Today we speak of coming out of the world and being not of the world; at that day, we need not say such words anymore. Nothing really matters much today, even the most spiritual work for the Lord is not *permanently* needed. Our one and only hope is to await the Lord's return. How can we be deeply rooted on earth? Does not the word of God test us all the time? The Lord is at the doors (see Matt. 24.33). Let us wait for His coming.

Is there any passage of Scripture which tells us whether the coming of the Lord is in Spirit or in His own person? The answer is that the Lord's return is physical and no longer only in Spirit. For is it not recorded in Acts that as the disciples were looking, the

Lord Jesus was taken up; and a cloud received Him out of their sight. And while they were looking stedfastly upward as He went, two men stood by them in white apparel, who declared: "Ye men of Galilee, why stand ye looking into heaven? this Jesus, who was received up from you into heaven, shall so come in like manner as ye beheld him going into heaven" (Acts 1.11). In addition, it is said in Matthew that "when the Son of man shall come in his glory, and all the angels with him, then shall he sit on the throne of his glory" (Matt. 25.31). Just as He went, so shall He come again. He went in a cloud, so shall He return in a cloud. He went visibly, and so He shall be seen in coming back. For He shall come back in a glorified body. As a matter of fact, He ascended as a real Man, a risen Man; in like manner shall He also return as a real, resurrected Man. His second coming will be just as real and factual as was His crucifixion.

The coming of the Lord will conclude this wicked generation and finally bring peace to this world. This present age is full of violence, and the smell of blood is nauseating. The entire world is covered with the dark cloud of war. The earth which was created with such beauty is now ruined beyond repair by the derangement of the devil and the sin of mankind. War is the horrible face of the wicked one as well as it being the sword to destroy human beings.

At the close of the First World War, mankind thirsted for world peace and signed all kinds of peace pacts and international agreements. Within twenty more years the Second World War had begun. Peace pacts are nothing more than blank notes. According to the booklet, "Give us Peace," during the past 3300 years, the world has concluded over 8,000 peace agreements. Nonetheless, its people cannot stop war nor bloodshedding. The average life of a peace pact lasts but half a year. When a peace agreement is abrogated, another war is fought: agreements made and agreements annulled. There is no real peace on earth. Only at the return of the Lord will there be lasting peace.

3 | Occupation*

> When we were with you, this we commanded you, If
> any will not work, neither let him eat. For we hear of some
> that walk among you disorderly, that work not at all, but
> are busybodies. Now them that are such we command and
> exhort in the Lord Jesus Christ, that with quietness they
> work, and eat their own bread. (2 Thess. 3.10-12)

1. Occupations Sanctioned in the Bible

The occupation of a Christian is a major consideration in life. If he or she chooses the wrong occupation,
that person will be hampered in his or her progress in
the Lord. Hence a Christian must be careful in the
choice of occupation.

---

*This message when given in 1948 at the Mount Kuling Conference
Center near Foochow, China was a timely one, in view of a special
situation then existing in China which seriously needed to be addressed on behalf of the Christians there. The same, however, may

At the time of creation, God not only created man but also planned for his occupation. He appointed Adam and Eve to dress and to keep the garden of Eden. Hence their job before the fall was that of a gardener.

After the fall, they had to toil with sweat in order to have bread, for the ground was cursed because of them. This indicates that after the fall the appointed occupation for man is that of a farmer. God knows better than anybody else that farming is the best pursuit for a fallen mankind.

From Genesis chapter 4 we find Cain was tilling the ground while Abel his brother was tending the sheep. Thus shepherding is added as another occupation besides that of being a farmer, and this is also acceptable to God.

As the earth's population began to increase, all sorts of craftsmen were raised up: the ironsmiths, the coppersmiths, the makers of musical instruments, and the manufacturers of sharp tools. And by the time of the building of the tower of Babel (see Gen. 11), there were masons and carpenters as well. Although the tower of Babel ought not to have been built, men nevertheless learned to build during that period.

From Genesis chapter 12 we learn that God chose

---

not be entirely or even partially applicable to the believers living within Western social and economic systems. The reader himself must judge. Yet the underlying principle advanced by the author in his message is nonetheless worthy of consideration; for although economic systems may indeed differ and local situations may doubtless vary, the basic points enunciated here can be of great help to those who seek to be led by the Spirit of God in choosing their occupations.—*Translator*

Abraham. And Abraham was a shepherd: he had many cattle and sheep. His grandson Jacob followed the same occupation—that of pasturing.

Later on we find the people of Israel making bricks in Egypt for Pharaoh. They were masons. But when they came out of Egypt, God gave them two blessings: one was to shepherd the flocks, and the other was to till the land of Canaan that was flowing with milk and honey. That a branch with a cluster of grapes took two men to carry clearly indicated the work of husbandry. That God warned that if they rebelled against Him and worshiped idols He would cause the heaven to be like brass and the earth as iron so that the ground would yield no produce, was further evidence that their main employments in the promised land of Canaan were to be farming and pasturing. The above are the various God-approved occupations shown in the Old Testament.

What about the basic occupations mentioned in the New Testament? From the parables spoken by the Lord Jesus we find that farming and pasturing are again the main occupations—Matthew 13, the parable of the sower; Matthew 20, the parable of the vineyard; Luke 17, the servant who serves the master at table after coming in from having ploughed or kept the sheep; and John 10, the Lord as the good shepherd who lays down His life for the sheep.

When the Lord called His twelve apostles, most of them were fishermen. Were any of them a tax-collector, the Lord would demand that he leave his post. To the fishermen among them, however, He said this: "I will make you fishers of men" (Matt. 4.19b). Consequently, fishing was also a God-approved vocation.

Luke was a physician (Col. 4.14a), and Paul was a tentmaker (Acts 18.3). Tentmaking is different from fishing, in that it is manufacturing work. Whereas farming is a direct work, the labor of spinning, weaving, cutting or tentmaking involves an additional step in the laboring process, and is therefore manufacturing work.

We may say that from the Old Testament to the New, God has made His arrangement for occupations. The disciples of the Lord were either farmers or shepherds or craftsmen or fishermen or manufacturers. We can add one more occupation, that of a laborer. For the New Testament does have this word: "the laborer is worthy of his [wages]" (1 Tim. 5.18). A laborer is one who works with his hands in unskilled or manual labor. Such employment is also sanctioned in the Bible.

2. The Principle Governing Occupations

In searching the Scriptures, we find that God has ordained for men various kinds of jobs. Underlying these occupations, there is a basic principle—which is, that men ought to be profited from nature through earning their hire by putting in either their time or their strength. Apart from this principle operating in any given occupation, the Bible does not seem to approve of any other kind of employment. Let us discuss several facets of this principle, as follows:

(a) *Draw Resources from Nature for the Increase of Wealth.* How are we to explain this statement? Perhaps we can best explain in this way: a sower sows his seed, and later he gets thirty or sixty or a hundred-fold yield. Such multiplication comes from the supply of nature which is abundant and open to all. For God causes the sun to shine on the unrighteous as well as on the righteous. He also causes rain to fall on them both. This is the advantage of farming. Since it is God who gives the increase, this shows that God's purpose is for men to take grace from nature. The same rule applies to pasturing. As one tends the flock, he is profited with many lambs as well as with wool and milk. This is production increase obtained from nature.

In the New Testament, we observe fishing as an occupation. To fish in the sea is still drawing resources from nature. No one will become poorer because I fish in the sea. I may get richer through fishing, but no one will become poorer for my sake. My sheep may give birth to six lambs and my cattle may beget two calves, yet no one will become poorer because of me. Or I may be farming and obtain an hundredfold increase. I certainly will not cause anyone or any family to suffer hunger or loss because of the good yield from my land. Thus the basic principle for human occupations is: *I gain but nobody will lose*. The noblest occupations as appointed by God come under this rule.

(b) *Manufacturing — the Increase of Value*. Paul's tentmaking comes under the same principle, though not without some variation. He does not make his profit by going directly to nature as in fishing, pasturing or farming; rather, he puts his effort and time into a kind of manufacturing work. We may view such work as that which increases the value. For example: A piece of cloth may be worth one dollar. If I cut it, sew it, and make it into a tent, it can be sold for, say, two dollars. But this means I increase its value and earn my wages.

Nobody will become poorer as a result of my earning a fair share. I simply increase the worth of this piece of cloth by adding my labor to it. It is therefore proper for me to earn my wages in this way. Such employment may be called a value-increasing occupation.

(c) *A Laborer's Wages.* In the case of an employee who works for another, or in the case of a mason or a physician, such a one is simply earning the wages derived from his own labor. Though he does not make his profit out of nature nor does he increase any value by means of manufacturing, he has nevertheless expended so much of his time and exerted so much of his strength that he is entitled to receive precisely that much in wages which is commensurate with his effort and time. God permits a laborer to have his share of wages.

3. The Choice of Occupation

There is one occupation towards which the Bible looks unfavorably, and that is the job of trading. This is something to which I wish to call your special attention. If it be possible, I would hope young believers would avoid this occupation. In order for us to have a clearer view, I shall enlarge upon this subject as follows. Suppose we have a hundred people here, each with a million dollars. The total amount of wealth is therefore a hundred million. Naturally, in trading we expect to make a profit; so now, let us say I am able to double my money within one month, that is to say, I double my original million to two millions. Ignoring the fact of whether I trade righteously or unrighteously, one thing is certain: if I make a million more, some among the one hundred men must have suffered loss in the process, that is to say, they will most likely each have less than a million dollars in their respective hands.

We are all Christians, and therefore brothers. Is it fitting for me to win your money? Is it right for me to be richer but you poorer? Even if my competitors are heathens, I myself am still a Christian. And hence as a child of God, I have the obligation to maintain a dignity and position that is in harmony with God's viewpoint. It is consequently unfitting for me to take advantage of not only other believers but of the unbelievers as well, however righteous may be the way I trade. Let us see that in trading, one particular situation is clearly unavoidable: that to transfer money from your pocket to mine, I have to make you suffer. This is a fact.

But in the occupations which God has ordained for men, such problem does not exist. For if I am farming, I shall harvest — say, a hundred loads of rice — without lessening what you have stored in your home, not even a pound less. No one will suffer because of my reaping a hundred loads of rice. We cannot call this profiteering; it is simply increasing the wealth of the land. We need to perceive the great difference between these two. God does not wish His children to set their minds on the one purpose of making profit. He wants us to take up employments which will increase wealth. This basic principle is quite simple and clear. Do not be occupied from morning till night with the one thought of making money. Keep well in mind instead that if you make money, somebody else must incur loss.

To increase my money is to decrease another's money. And this is what we call trading.

Hence we have to choose among these three kinds of occupation: trading, laboring, and producing. The noblest occupation as sanctioned by God in the Bible is that of production, for in production I increase the wealth without at the same time making others poor. If after a few years of pasturing I increase my flock from a hundred to four hundred, I indeed have an increase, but no one else will have experienced a decrease because of me; for I have only increased the wealth directly from nature.

It is not so, however, with trading. For instance, I buy a hundred sheep in one place and transport them for sale to another place. In the process of selling them I make ten dollars on every sheep, and thus I have a net profit of a thousand dollars. This money I gain without my having produced one sheep more. With the result that the world is not any the richer in its wealth because of me, and what is even worse, some people have even suffered *loss* because of my trading. Trading simply means *profiteering without production;* I increase my own money, but I do not increase the wealth of the world.*

From the standpoint of God's word, trading is the lowest form of all employments. If opportunity is given us to choose our occupation, may we choose that which will increase wealth or value rather than that which only

---

*This is in no way overlooking the law of availability as supplied by transporting goods from one place to another. It simply illustrates the absence of the basic principles of increasing wealth or increasing value.—*Translator*

increases our money. It is very selfish if we choose the latter.

4. The Increase of Value

The principle underlying an employment such as Paul's tentmaking is somewhat different from the first category mentioned earlier — that of the increase of the world's wealth — yet still approved of God. Now in making a tent, it is quite true that there is no increase in cotton, or yarn, or cloth. Yet by cutting and sewing, by spending time on the cloth, it does increase the value of the raw material. According to Biblical scholars, the tents made during Paul's time were dyed. So that Dean Alford suggests that when Paul said "these hands" (Acts 20.34), he in effect was showing hands that had been heavily colored from dyes. In his making tents, therefore, Paul had to cut, to sew, and to dye.

It is good and quite acceptable to increase wealth, but it is also good and acceptable to increase value. It is good, for example, for me to make a chair out of a piece of wood; for in so doing, I have increased the value of the wood. Although I have not by this process increased wealth out of nature, I have nonetheless added one more chair to this world for its use. And thus I have made profit without having hurt anybody else. And such an occupation as this is therefore also permitted by God.

Hence we ought to uphold one or the other of two standards to our various occupations: *we must either increase the world's wealth or increase the value of things.*

5. Dealing with Pure Commerce

I too have studied a little economics and I know the necessity there is for trading in the world. But I am a Christian, not an economist. The Lord Jesus did indeed say, "Trade ye herewith till I come" (Luke 19.13b). The meaning of the Lord's word here, however, is that He wishes to have us as fully occupied with our works as the traders are with their businesses. We know that a trader is completely engrossed with the intention of making money. Wherever there is a chance to make money, the trader will take full advantage of it. So that what the Lord is saying here amounts to His desire for His followers to miss no chance but to seize upon every opportunity. In other words, we are to apply our whole heart to the work.

I suppose we all know that trading became quite prominent with Tyre and will end with Babylon of Revelation 18. Commencing with Ezekiel 28 we are told in the Scriptures that the one who symbolized trading was the king of Tyre who actually represented Satan: "By the abundance of thy traffic [trade] they filled the midst of thee with violence, and thou hast sinned" (Ez. 28.16a). We would therefore do well to keep in mind that that occupation which aims at making a profit at another's expense and not increasing the world's wealth is not God's appointed employment for His children. It is rather a satanic employment, in that it works according to an evil principle.

Trading follows the evil principle of getting another's money. When the money in my pocket increases, that in the other's pocket is decreased. Suppose, for instance, that there are 4 billion people in this world, and that the total world's wealth is 20 billion dollars. If anyone desires to make money through trading, the consequence flowing from that action will be very simple. Where there is an increase of one's money, there will be a corresponding decrease of another's money. For the total amount of the world's money supply is limited. Now to increase one's money at the expense of another —this is called pure commerce. I do not suggest that we should not sell the fish we catch, nor the wheat we harvested, nor the tents we make. We may indeed sell them, but such trading activities as these are not pure commerce. Why? because we exchange our *products* for money, and our profits are made from *nature*. We do not rob from others to make ourselves rich.

A basic Christian notion is that God's people should not ever rob others. For a believer—who has been endowed with such a high and noble position of being a child of God—to make a profit out of the people of the world is unquestionably something that looks bad. If the head of our government should come to Mount Kuling and find that the mountain people were suffering from malaria, would he sell them quinine tablets in such a way as to make for himself a personal profit? Could he or would he make money from a coolie? No, considering his position, such an act would be outrageous. Let me tell you that it would be even more outrageous and shameful were a Christian to make a profit at the expense of others.

We Christians have our noble position and dignity. It is therefore a disgraceful thing for us to profit from another's loss. We should not enrich ourselves at all by pure commerce. We ought rather to be farmers who till and plant, for God has so ordained nature to yield its increase. It would be far more glorious to do that than to take another's money by means of pure commerce.

Where, then, lies our course? We ought to increase either the number or the value of a thing. Such an occupation is approved of God. Pure commerce is not accepted by Him. Special attention should be paid to what is recorded in Ezekiel 28, for the principle of profiting by trading was first illustrated in the Bible by the king of Tyre. And the Lord reproached him, saying: "By the abundance of thy traffic [trade] . . . thou hast sinned." The source of commerce is wrong. We then come to Revelation 18 which shows us what the judgment of Babylon will be at the closing of this world and the beginning of the kingdom to come. There the merchants of the earth, after the lapse of many centuries since the time of Ezekiel 28, shall weep and mourn for Babylon. Of the merchandise they handle, "gold" heads the list and the "souls of men" conclude it (vv.12,13). From gold to human souls, these merchants will have traded and trafficked in everything possible. Their sole aspiration will have been to make a profit and to get rich. For this reason, brothers and sisters in Christ should flee from this the basest of all employments.

Yet here we must distinguish between pure commerce and productive commerce. Trading of production is permitted, but pure buying and selling through the commercial exchanges and other such practices is absolutely unacceptable to God. It is right for a brother to sell what he has produced in the field, but for him to buy rice in order to sell it at a higher price is objectionable. Though both are selling, they are vastly different the one from the other. If I make a tent at night and sell it the next day, I am engaged in the same kind of work as was Paul; but if I buy ten tents today and then sell them tomorrow, I am involved in a different kind of work than what Paul was involved in. To sell what you have labored in is blessed by the Lord, but the buying and selling of commodities as a kind of middleman has nothing in view but profiteering. From the Christian and Biblical standpoint, the latter is the lowest of all occupations. Aside from making a profit for oneself, it does not help the national life at all.

He who is engaged in *pure* commerce should not be a responsible brother in the church. For such a person can hardly be expected to be freed from the power or influence of money. Our way is clear: God's children cannot serve unless they are wholly liberated from the influence of money. If they are still bound by money, the church will have no more future. We therefore must choose the right occupation.

Should brothers and sisters pay special attention to their occupations, the church will be spared many trials if the Lord should delay His return. Henceforth our mentality will undergo a total change: it will not be a matter of how much money we make, but one of how we can do the things which are pleasing to God.

6. The Noblest Occupation

Shepherds and farmers are productive people, whereas merchants are non-productive. In between are workers and laborers such as physicians, nurses, masons, factory-workers, and others. They put in their labor, and so their employment is also considered to be a good one in the Bible. Although they do not produce, they nonetheless take nothing away from others. They make their profit neither from nature nor from other people. They use their time, physical strength and brain power in exchange for that which can provide them with the necessities of life. A worker or laborer is worthy of his wages. The noblest of all is still a productive occupation; and the next is a working occupation.

Productive people profit from nature but take nothing from men; working people take neither from nature nor from men; whereas trading people take nothing from nature but do make a profit at the expense of men. These three are distinctive in their respective character. The productive ones have the noblest of all occupations, for they seek their profit solely from nature. The working class earn their wages through either their strength or their brain or both. Yet their gain will still not make anybody else the poorer for it. Only the traders are engaged in the lowest employment because they make their gain exclusively through depriving their fellowmen.

7. The Way before Us

Before we conclude our discussion, we need to recognize the need to be moderate when it comes to speaking out about the consequences that logically should flow from our assessment of this matter. We should not indiscriminately condemn brothers who are middlemen or merchants, for they may not have had the opportunity to choose their occupation for themselves. Yet we do hope that they may hereafter be able to change their occupation. I know a man who was a good Christian brother when he left school. But not long after he joined himself to the commercial world, his heart was corrupted. He thought of nothing but profiteering. If he was asked to purchase anything, he would try his best to make some profit out of it. I say again that his heart was corrupted. And that is why we hope no brother will choose to be engaged in pure commerce.

Because pure commerce is not a Biblically acceptable employment, I would hope that after ten or twenty years we would have our mentality so completely transformed that no one would choose to be a trader. We who are believers should rather choose to teach than to trade, to work with our hands than to buy and sell. It is of course right for us to sell the produce we get from our farmland or from our pasture, or to sell the product we make as finished goods by means of our added work. The more of our labor we put in, the more we will be blessed of God.

Today we are poor; beware lest we become rich. For I must acknowledge that it is actually not hard for us to get rich because we as believers are honest and diligent, and because we do not waste our money in smoking and drinking and luxurious living. Do remember that before John Wesley died he said that he was deeply concerned with the Wesleyans for they would soon become the wealthiest people in the world since they were honest, diligent, and thrifty. And his prediction has indeed come true: the Wesleyans are wealthy, but are they rich in God?

In conclusion, let me say that we expect young believers to earn their money with honest labor. Do not aim at making a great deal by means of buying and selling. Our principle must always be to increase wealth but not money. And thus the money we earn will be clean, and it will be blessed as it is offered to God. The rule, then, is to labor or to produce. Although we dare not forbid trading, we nevertheless maintain that we should try our best to avoid pure commerce. It is a base employment which can easily drown a Christian in destruction and pierce him through with many sorrows (1 Tim. 6.9,10).

PART THREE

THE FULLNESS OF GOD'S SALVATION

1 | The Righteousness of God

At the outset, let me ask two questions: (1) Are we, as children of God, saved by the righteousness of the Lord Jesus? And (2) How many times is the righteousness of Jesus mentioned in the New Testament? To answer the second question first, we shall find that in the entire New Testament the righteousness of Jesus is only mentioned once—in 2 Peter 1.1: "Simon Peter, bondman and apostle of Jesus Christ, to them that have received like precious faith with us through the righteousness of our God and Saviour Jesus Christ" (Darby).

In answer to the first question, therefore, it is not accurate to say that we are justified by the righteousness of the Lord Jesus. For His own righteousness only gives Him a position before God as that of His being worthy to be our Savior. If the righteousness of Jesus were able to save us, then the cross would not be indispensable. His righteousness is the righteousness He had while He was living on earth before His crucifixion.

We are not saved by His personal righteousness, but by the righteousness which He accomplished before God on the cross for us.

To put it more clearly, we are saved through His death. Otherwise, His living would condemn us rather than justify us. For He is the beloved Son of God and He is without blemish. But we are sinners destined to be cursed. His righteousness would expose us before God as our being even more worthy to be condemned.

It is quite amazing to find in the Bible that we are saved by the righteousness of God. This is repeatedly presented in Romans chapters 1 and 3. Hence let us take note that it is not the righteousness of Jesus, but the righteousness of God, that saves us as Romans 3 makes clear:

> Because by the works of the law shall no flesh be justified in his sight; for through the law cometh the knowledge of sin. But now apart from the law a righteousness of God hath been manifested, being witnessed by the law and the prophets; even the righteousness of God through faith in Jesus Christ unto all them that believe; for there is no distinction; for all have sinned, and fall short of the glory of God . . . Christ Jesus: whom God set forth to be a propitiation, through faith, in his blood, to show his righteousness because of the passing over of the sins done aforetime, in the forbearance of God; for the showing, I say, of his righteousness at this present season: that he might himself be just, and the justifier of him that hath faith in Jesus. (vv. 20–23,24b–26)

The righteousness of God, to my understanding,

must follow the nature of God. For God to do anything, He must maintain His own nature in whatever He does. What, then, is the righteousness of God? What is His nature? Frankly, as sinners we do not care how we are saved so long as we *are* saved. But God is righteous. Even in saving us, He has to defend His righteous nature. He cannot carelessly forgive our sins. Whatever method He uses to save us, He cannot deny himself. If a method chosen were to conflict with His nature, it just could not be done that way. Though God is able to use such a method, He would not do so because such a way of saving us would make Him unrighteous. Unlike man, He would not in any way compromise himself in saving us.

Honestly speaking, we as sinners could not care less about the manner by which we are to be saved. Yet if we are really people with discipline, we too will declare it is not right for God to save us indiscriminately. The way He uses to save us must not fall short of His glory. Otherwise, we would be found thanking God for saving us, but at the same time we would say that He is a careless God. Instead, we want God to be true to His own Self as well as we want ourselves to be saved. Although this creates a dilemma, this is the only way to make salvation trustworthy.

Something very interesting happened in Nanking, and I love to relate this story. Once a missionary asked me to preach in Nanking University. As I arrived at the campus, the chancellor himself came to receive me. This man had such a menacing face that students dared not face him. We entered the chapel together, and he chaired the meeting. It so happened that a vase stood on the pulpit. So, in the course of my preaching, I used an illustration by asking the chancellor, "What would be done if a student were to break this vase?" "According to school regulations," replied the chancellor, "he must reimburse the University eighty dollars." "What if he did not have the money?" I asked. "He must reimburse the University whether he has the money or not," the chancellor insisted. "Suppose you especially liked that student," I proceeded; "could you then say to him, Because I like you very much, you do not need to reimburse the school?" "Nothing of the sort," answered the chancellor, "because according to University regulations it must still be reimbursed!" No matter how much the chancellor loved that student, he could not compromise the school laws; otherwise, all the vases in the school might end up being broken.

We can easily discern that all the vases would end up being broken due to the accommodation of the chancellor. If he really wanted to help the situation, he should so help that it would cause no trouble for himself. Similarly, in this matter of saving people, God does so in such a way that not only will man simply praise Him and not blaspheme Him as well, but also the devil will have his mouth clamped shut.

Then I said to the chancellor, "Suppose this vase were already broken, and according to school regulations the University must be reimbursed in the sum of eighty dollars. Yet you love this student, but he has no money. What, then, would you do?" "Well, . . ." he hesitated. So I pressed him, saying, "What would you do at that moment?" "This would be most difficult," he replied. "If you really loved that student," I continued, "and at the same time you did not want to break the school regulation, then would you not say to him that he must reimburse the broken vase with eighty dollars, but you would then rush home, take eighty dollars out of your own account, and give them to him and tell him to reimburse the University with the money? And thus the law would not be compromised and the person would be helped."

Nobody could then say anything because the student would have reimbursed according to University regulations. Now this could rightly be called the righteousness of the chancellor. And such is the way that God also treats us. We have sinned and God is just. He loves us, yet He cannot save us unjustly. "Therefore," says God, "I will give you My Son; through Him you may be saved." Do we now see how this is true salvation? Salvation does not just mean God saves us; it means that He gives His Son to us. Though we have sinned and fallen short of the glory of God, we may nonetheless bring God's Son to God as our recompense.

Strangely, a few days after I had spoken in the University chapel, the vase in question was broken. The face of the chancellor showed the marks of unhappiness. I asked him, "Will you demand reimbursement?" His answer was "Yes."

If the chancellor had no regard for affection, this matter could easily be settled according to the school regulations. But God loves us. He too would have no problem if He did not love us. Yet He has both a great affection towards us and is unwilling to do anything against His own nature.

What is salvation? Salvation means that though I

am a sinner, I can come before God through His Son. Hence we are saved not by the righteousness of the Lord Jesus but by His fulfilling the righteousness of God. Because the Lord Jesus is righteous, He is thus qualified to be our Savior.

Once a few seminary students came to me. They had just graduated after three years' study of the Bible. I like to challenge young believers with Bible questions. So I asked them, "Are we saved by the righteousness of God? Which is more secure—to be saved by the righteousness of God or by the love of God?" "Love," they answered with one accord. "Not so," I said; "it is not very secure if we are saved by the love of God."

Lacking love is not sin, but lacking righteousness is quite serious. If we are saved by love, God may love us this year, and so we are saved this year; but He may not love us next year, and then we become unsaved that year. But if we are saved by righteousness, God cannot be unrighteous. If it is only through love that God saves us, He may say "I do not love anymore," and we can do nothing about it.

Suppose you break the vase at your university. Can your chancellor take you to a back room and assure you by saying, "According to the school regulations you must reimburse the university for the vase you have broken; but never mind, I like you; just you keep quiet and I will also keep quiet about it"? Let me tell you that if I were the one who broke the vase, then each time I saw the chancellor, my heart would tremble because he might change his mind and ask for a reimbursement! If, however, he were to give me the eighty dollars with which I could then reimburse the school,

I could walk away confidently. It would not matter who gave me the money, just as long as I would have been able to reimburse the university according to its regulations. For once the chancellor, or whoever, has given me the money, he cannot retrieve it because the money would have already been used to reimburse the school. Even so with respect to salvation, as we depend on the righteousness which the Lord Jesus has accomplished, God is bound to forgive us no matter what His mood may be thereafter!

So that ultimately we are saved by the righteousness of God and not by the love of God. With this understanding, our hearts can be at rest and we can praise our righteous God.

May God forgive me — and may you all excuse me — for saying rather boldly that after the cross has become an accomplished fact we will be saved even if God is unwilling to save us. Our salvation does not depend upon how we think nor even upon what God thinks. Make no mistake about it, that after the money has been repaid — that is to say, after you are saved — you cannot be unsaved even if you were to repent, since the fruit of salvation has already been produced.

Thus salvation is established on righteousness, not on love. We are saved because God is righteous. It is indeed true that the love of God is that which moves Him to give His Son to us. And now through His Son we are able to approach God. This is the righteousness of God. Love leads to the cross, and the cross leads to righteousness. God's love causes Him to give us His Son; God's righteousness enables us to approach God through His Son.

Before the cross, it is a matter of God's love; *after* the cross, it is a matter of God's righteousness. After we are saved, nothing can change the fact, neither man nor even God. The case is settled.

God has saved us apart from the law. Let us read again Romans 3.21-26:

> But now apart from the law a righteousness of God hath been manifested, being witnessed by the law and the prophets; even the righteousness of God through faith in Jesus Christ unto all them that believe; for there is no distinction; for all have sinned, and fall short of the glory of God; being justified freely by his grace through the redemption that is in Christ Jesus: whom God set forth to be a propitiation, through faith, in his blood, to show his righteousness because of the passing over of the sins done aforetime, in the forbearance of God; for the showing, I say, of his righteousness at this present season: that he might himself be just, and the justifier of him that hath faith in Jesus.

As soon as you see the righteousness of God, your problem is solved. After God has saved us, even He cannot say He has not saved us, because He is a righteous person. He cannot be unrighteous. Therefore, no one enters heaven by stealth. Today, our salvation and our entry into heaven is something which neither the angels nor the devil can gainsay. This is because our forgiveness and salvation are based on the righteousness of God.

It is thus evident that we are saved not because we have good works nor because we have kept God's law. Some will probably say that if we are not saved by keeping the law, then we have no need to keep the law. Let us read verses 27, 28, and 31: "Where then is the glorying? It is excluded. By what manner of law? of works? Nay; but by a law of faith. We reckon therefore that a man is justified by faith apart from the works of the law. . . . Do we then make the law of none effect through faith? God forbid: nay, we establish the law." Paul declares a very forceful "No" to this idea: we not only cannot overthrow the law, we also rather establish the law by our faith in the Lord Jesus.

Let me illustrate this matter of the law as follows. I have broken the flower vase. I have sinned and thus have broken the law. But I can still insist that I have *kept* the law. For there are two alternatives in keeping the law. For example, either I buy a ticket before I board a bus, or according to the regulation of the bus company I pay double after I alight from the bus; for the latter method likewise establishes the law. If none of us has bought the required ticket, we have to accept the penalty of paying double. Upon our arrival, we cannot climb out of the window and escape, because this is not allowed by the bus company. And hence we establish that particular law of the company by accepting the penalty.

There is none in the world who has kept the law of God, for all of us have sinned. Thank God, though, He gave His Son to us. Although we have sinned, we have the Son who is God's reimbursement for us.

Today we establish the law by trusting in God. No matter what Satan may say to us, we know we have God's Son who has suffered the penalty of sin for us.

The law says that whoever sins must be punished. Thank God, His Son was punished for me. And we are saved because the Son of God has been judged for us. So that when I accept the Lord Jesus, I accept the righteousness of God. I come to God through the Lord Jesus. I see the love of God in His giving His Son to me, and I am not fearful of the righteousness of God anymore because in spite of the fact that my sins must be punished, God cannot deny that He has already received the recompense from my hands — namely, that I bring God's Son to Him as my recompense, since He has given His Son to me.

Once there were two sisters around the age of twelve. When a Christian brother inquired about their salvation, the one who was a little older replied, "I am saved by the grace of God"; but the younger one answered, "I am continuously saved by the righteousness of God." I feel their answers are marvelous: they are answers which are not taught by man.

God's righteousness suffers no change. Hence, no matter what may happen to us, and regardless of what we ourselves may think, the fact that we are saved remains unchanged. Whatever attempts to shake our salvation are attempts to shake God's righteousness. Thank the Lord, no one can make God unrighteous. How, then, can any child of God cease to praise Him?

In saving us, God gives us a handle to grasp hold of, and this handle is the cross. By having the cross we have nothing to fear. Suppose we are to perish; we may say to God, "What about the cross?" Let me tell you, He must respect the cross. He gave to us His Son who has died for us, and by His Son we come before Him. This is the righteousness of God.

That the righteousness of the Lord Jesus saves us

is not taught in the New Testament. What the Bible says is that the righteousness of God saves us. The righteousness of the Lord Jesus belongs to Him alone and it gives Him a place before God. His own personal righteousness is not directly related to us. When we put on the robe of righteousness, we in actuality are putting on the Lord Jesus himself and not the righteousness of the Lord Jesus. The Scriptures teach that the Lord Jesus himself is made to be our robe of righteousness (cf. 1 Cor. 1.30) so that by Him we may be justified before God. It is not by His personal righteousness being made our righteousness. We approach God through Jesus himself, not through Jesus' righteousness being reckoned as our righteousness.

This righteousness of God means that in saving us He has manifested that He is righteous. How do we become righteous? By having our debt paid. Thus the penalty we should have received is already borne by Another. We are not like a prisoner who escapes from the prison unwatched. No, our penalty is paid, so today we are justified.

You may ask why we are now just. By way of response let me use an illustration: Suppose you are a thief who tries to pick a person's pocket on the bus. You are discovered and caught. You are brought to the court, and the judge asks you if you have picked anyone's pocket. You say, Yes. The judge then says that you must return what you have stolen. If the stolen goods are still in your possession, you can easily restore them. But if they are no longer there, you are required to pay a hundred dollars as damages. What if you do not have the hundred dollars? Even if—without immediately repaying the damage—you are allowed to go, you will try to avoid the plaintiff if ever you see him on the street, lest he give you trouble. But if you *have* paid the damages, you will not flee when you see him because he cannot ask you to pay the second time. Likewise in spiritual terms, here I am a sinner; but when I see God, He cannot ask me to pay again because it has already been paid by the Lord Jesus for me. I am now a just man, a justified sinner.

We have sinned, but through the Lord Jesus we are now justified before God. Justification means that through the Lord Jesus, who has received God's wrath in my stead, I am now a just man before God. Today as I come before Him by the Lord Jesus, I will be declared as righteous before Him. By nature I am a thief; in history, I am a thief; but I have the hundred dollars paid. If God refuses to accept the hundred dollars, I am still a sinner. Once He accepts the payment, however, I am no longer a sinner.

The righteousness of the Lord Jesus qualifies Him to be our Savior. As He fulfills righteousness on the cross, He is able to save us. The righteousness of God is manifested when we come to Him through Christ Jesus.

2 | The Word "Sin" in Romans

We have seen the righteousness of God and this matter of justification; now we will continue on with the subject: from what does God save us? We have dealt with the positive aspect of salvation; now we will deal with its negative aspect. On the one side is the righteousness of God; on the other side is sin.

In the New Testament, sin is viewed from two different angles. It is differentiated by the singular and plural numbers. The basis for the difference lies between the issue of knowledge and that of conduct. The two writers who touch upon the word "sin" most are Paul and John. In using the word "sin," John usually uses the singular number, though he sometimes uses the plural number also. Paul employs the word "sin" in both numbers. When he uses "sins" he is pointing us to the sins that we have committed, which can be counted. In other words, he refers to outward deeds.

But there is "sin" in the singular which points to our very life. For we may not only commit many sins outwardly, we have within us the source of sin. Notice how clearly Paul distinguishes the words "sins" and "sin." One is related to sinful deeds, the other is related to the sinner himself. If you were to ask a child, Who is a sinner?, his answer would be, Whoever commits sin is a sinner. But those who know the Bible will answer differently. The Bible does not say that one who sins becomes a sinner; rather, it says that because we are sinners, therefore we commit one sin after another. I am a Chinese; therefore I speak Chinese. Yet I cannot presume to say that all who speak Chinese are Chinese. Now Paul is most careful in the use of the word "sin." Whenever he uses "sins" plural he means sinful deeds that are committed. I commit "sins" plural because I have that "sin" singular in me. Whether I am a sinner or not is decided by that source of sin in me. With the root of sin in me, I bring forth many sins.

The book of Romans speaks of sin on the one hand and of righteousness on the other. The first eight chapters are doctrinal in nature and they are divided into two parts. What precedes 5.12 is one section, what follows 5.12 is another. The first section deals with justification (being "reckoned for righteousness" — 4.3,22); the second section deals with being "made righteous" (5.19). The former is forgiveness after having committed many sins; the latter is deliverance. Before 5.12, we do not find the word "sinner," since all we see are sins committed. After 5.12, however, it is no longer sins committed but the sinner himself that is in view.

When an evangelist quotes the words in Romans 3.23, "For all have sinned," does he mean all are sinners? Remember that the word "sinner" is not directly addressed to a sinner; the words "have sinned" are aimed at sinners. Accurately speaking, a sinner is not qualified to know that he is a sinner. He does not see his real self. Is it all right for a poor man to steal? What do you call such an act? Here we see that Paul at this point only talks about "have sinned," not about "sinner." The phrase "for all have sinned" refers instead to sins committed rather than to the sinners themselves. At that juncture, a person only knows he has committed sins; he has no idea that he is a sinner. This knowledge comes after he has failed hundreds of times; only then will he realize he is a sinner.

Many confess themselves to be sinners. This is really a simplification. For at that time they only know they have sinned; they do not see themselves as sinners, as people who are born of sin. When Paul says that all have sinned, he is referring to sin in the plural number, for one has not yet seen sin in its singular number. Rarely has anyone at the time of his salvation been enlightened to see himself as born of sin. David once declared, "They [mine iniquities] are more than the hairs of my head" (Ps. 40.12). People ordinarily see only "sins" committed. Therefore God deals first with sin in the plural number. The blood of His Son cleanses us from all our sins. Hence in the first section of Romans 1-8, the basic focus lies in getting rid of sins through forgiveness. It does not speak of anything else. Yet the second section no longer mentions the blood, but only the cross. For blood deals with sins whereas the cross deals with the sinner. There is no cross in the first section; there is no blood in the second. On this side is forgiveness, on the other side is deliverance. What God has clearly distinguished, let no man confuse.

Once in Shanghai a missionary testified by saying, "God forgives all my sin." To him I said, "Brother, you say something which is unscriptural, because the Bible never says 'forgive sin'." "What is the difference?" he asked. "There is a great difference," I replied, "for it is impossible to forgive sin in the singular number. When I have done wrong, I need forgiveness. And I can only be forgiven with God's righteous provision. But the sin within me is a power. It remains the same whether or not my sins are forgiven. God delivers me from sin by having it crucified. It is done with, not by cutting off fingers, but by cutting off the head. We lay under the power of sin, but the section after 5.12 shows us that our old man was crucified with Christ. The way is clearly marked. There are two things that are troubling me: one is sinful deeds, the other is the root of sin within. For the one there is forgiveness through the blood; for the other there is deliverance through the cross. I was crucified, and a dead person is delivered from the law of sin." We must notice the difference between "sin" and "sins."

Now when John uses the word "sin" he has an additional meaning for it which Paul does not have. This also is a point which all who study the Bible should notice. In many instances, John uses the words "sins" and "sin" in the same way as Paul does. But in 1 John 1.7, the word "sin" is singular. We would think that Paul would certainly use "sins" in the plural here. Again in verse 8, the "sin" is singular. But in verse 9, the plural word "sins" is used twice, just as Paul would use it, for they both refer to the sinful deeds which are committed. Actually the word "sin" in verse 8 is used in the same way that Paul uses it in the second section of Romans (5.12-8). It tells of the presence of sin. What John is contesting there is not that there are those who are saying that they have not sinned but saying that they have no sin. That, for John, is a lie.

The only difference in use is found in verse 7, where John writes: "and the blood of Jesus his Son cleanseth us from all sin." If this verse is speaking of the sin principle, then the root of sin cannot be cleansed by the blood. A similar use by John is found in John 1.29: "Behold, the Lamb of God, that taketh away the sin of the world!" According to our thinking, the Lamb of God takes away the "sins" plural of the world. Consequently, there must be an additional meaning of "sin"—that it refers to the *problem* of sin.

The Lord Jesus came to solve this problem of sin. As the Lamb of God, He bore our sins in His body on the cross; thus, He has completely solved this problem of sin. If we walk in the light as God is in the light, we have fellowship one with another, and the blood of Jesus God's Son cleanses us from all our sin.

What is this light? In the Bible there are two different kinds of light spoken of: one is holiness, the other is the gospel. Does the light in this connection refer to holiness or to the gospel? Light is the opposite of darkness on the one hand, and the opposite of being hidden on the other. Is the light here in contrast to darkness or to a being hidden? If the light points to holiness, listen to the way it would read: "But if we walk in holiness as he is in holiness, we have fellowship one with another." We would of course have fellowship, but the words following ("and the blood of Jesus his Son cleanseth us from all sin") would seem to be out of context. Hence the light here must be the revelation of the gospel.

If we walk in the light of the gospel, we know how God's Son has come as a man and died for men. God no longer hides himself behind the veil. In the Old Testament time, all was conjecture because God was hidden. Today God has revealed himself. If we know the God of light, the blood of His Son Jesus cleanses us from all sin. Thus, the special use of "sin" in the singular by John is cleared up. I trust we now see that both "sin" and "sins" are solved forever.

Daniel Steele was one of the best among the Methodists in the nineteenth century. He was a good friend of J. N. Darby, yet he sometimes could not stand the latter's grand view of the gospel. One day Darby was commenting that if we walk in the light of the gospel, the blood of Jesus God's Son cleanses us from all sin. He declared that today God is in the light, and if we hear the gospel today, we too walk in the light of the gospel. As we live by the light of God, the blood of Jesus God's Son will doubtlessly cleanse us from all sin. Steele could not accept Darby's premise that the gospel is everything. So he raised a question: "Darby, what will happen if a person does not walk towards the light?" "Then God's light," replied Darby, "will shine on his back." So the problem lies not in how holy a person is before his sin is cleansed. God is the God of love. If I walk in His light, He cleanses my sin. If I turn my back to His light, His light still shines. This is the gospel from which there is no escape. Do we now see how the problem of sin is solved? In me there is something called sin, and out from me sins are being committed.

Paul in his epistles always makes a clear distinction between sin and sins. In 2 Corinthians 5.21 he writes this: "Him who knew no sin he made to be sin on our behalf; that we might become the righteousness of God in him." The use of the word "sin" is similar to the way John uses it. God makes Him who has "no sin," not Him who has "no sins." For the Lord Jesus is not only without sins, He is also without sin. One day the Lord Jesus became "sin" for us, not became "sins" for us. For on that day He is made the whole problem of sin before God on our behalf. As God deals with Jesus, He deals with the basic problem of "sin."

Let us return to Romans. When a person first believes in the Lord, all he can understand is that he is too dirty, that he speaks too much, so that he cannot lift up his head before God. Hence in the first section—that part before 5.12—the emphasis is on "sins": how sin after sin after sin is being washed away. Though at that time the person may also confess himself to be a sinner because of his defilement and pride, his knowledge of being a sinner born of sin is nonetheless very limited.

The Bible teaches much more clearly about the sinner. Becaue sin is within me, therefore I lose my temper. That which is in me always causes me to sin. Thus I am convinced that I am truly a sinner. It takes many rounds of experiencing Romans 7 before I begin to see one day that no matter how I try I just cannot be "good," because I am a sinner. I may sense my face being covered with clay. And I thank God that there is a mirror. So I confess I have sinned, and ask the Lord Jesus to cleanse me. But I only see I am *covered* with clay; I do not yet realize that I *am made* of clay. I may count a thousand sins and have them all cleansed before God. But I am made of clay. The more I am washed, the dirtier I become. Do you not know that you are born of sin and that it is you your *self* who needs to be dealt with? Before God you need not only to ask for cleansing, but also to ask for deliverance from your self.

So on the one side is this question of sinful deeds. Hebrews 10 shows us that we may be so cleansed as to have our conscience void of offense. On the other side, as sinners, we need the cross to deliver us. A sinner is therefore in need of deliverance as well as of salvation. A person who sins needs to be forgiven, and the same person, being a sinner, needs to be delivered.

How clear are the words in Romans 7.7,8: "What shall we say then? Is the law sin? God forbid. Howbeit, I had not known sin, except through the law: for I had not known coveting, except the law had said, Thou shalt not covet: but sin, finding occasion, wrought in me through the commandment all manner of coveting: for apart from the law sin is dead." Only after repeated failures do I cease to count the number of sins I commit. For the whole problem lies in the fact that I am undone. I begin to see through myself. It is now no longer a matter of committing one or more sins outwardly. Even if I say a few good words, I am still a sinner born of sin.

Do keep in mind that when you first know sin, it is always in terms of a countable number of outward incorrect actions or words. But later on, you begin to see that your whole being is sin. I am indeed cleansed by the blood of Jesus, yet I am sold under sin, I am totally undone. What follows after Romans 7.7,8 reveals this fact: "For that which I do I know not: for not what I would, that do I practise; but what I hate, that I do" (Rom. 7.15); "for I know that in me, that is, in my flesh, dwelleth no good thing" (7.18).

Hence the problem of sin is not an external one; rather, it is an internal problem. In the beginning we may say that though our deeds are sinful, our heart is good. As we come to know the Lord more, however, we come to say that even though our deeds may be good, our heart is bad. From the plural we move to the singular. A believer must first deal with his sins item by item. For without such dealings, he will never be able to see sin in its singular number. May we always ask the Lord to cause us to see. May God bless these simple words.

3 | Original Sin

And the man knew Eve his wife; and she conceived, and bare Cain, and said, I have gotten a man with the help of Jehovah. And again she bare his brother Abel. And Abel was a keeper of sheep, but Cain was a tiller of the ground. And in process of time it came to pass, that Cain brought of the fruit of the ground an offering unto Jehovah. And Abel, he also brought of the firstlings of his flock and of the fat thereof. And Jehovah had respect unto Abel and to his offering: but unto Cain and to his offering he had not respect. And Cain was very wroth, and his countenance fell. And Jehovah said unto Cain, Why art thou wroth? and why is thy countenance fallen? If thou doest well, shall it not be lifted up? and if thou doest not well, sin coucheth at the door; and unto thee shall be its desire; but do thou rule over it. And Cain told Abel his brother. And it came to pass, when they were in the field, that Cain rose up against Abel his brother, and slew him. (Gen. 4.1–8)

What is the meaning of sacrifice? One aspect of its meaning is that God's attitude towards a sacrifice is His attitude towards the offerer. Sacrifice is symbolic. In rejecting a sacrifice, God rejects the person who offers it. In Hebrews 11.4 we read that Abel saw Christ. He came to God through Christ. He saw Christ in the lamb that he offered from his flock, and God also saw Christ in the lamb. Cain, on the other hand, being a tiller of the ground, forgot that sin was already in him. He ignored the fact that Adam had sinned. He might even have said to himself, "I have not killed, nor have I done any unrighteous thing." So Cain offered to God what he himself reckoned as good. He was confident that God would accept his sacrifice.

Yet Cain did not realize that it was not just a matter of whether or not he had sinned. This man was spiritually dull, proud, and blind. He completely overlooked the fact that something was wrong in man's relationship with God. He might have thought to himself that even though Adam had sinned, he had not sinned; so what? He did not know that "through one man sin entered into the world" (Rom. 5.12). This one man is Adam, and this sin is original sin. Cain viewed himself as having kept up with his conscience from his youth. He therefore came to God without fear and trembling. He forgot that mankind had sinned before God and that sin was already in the world.

Once I had a conversation with a Moslem. He suggested that what we both believed and worshiped was the same God. Yet this was the way I answered him: "Most people do not have a good feeling towards God. Even if they do, they cannot worship Him in their sins, because God is a holy God. The Moslems say they can come to God by their good works. To use a colloquial illustration: you may wish to have a wealthy man be your godfather, but what if he refuses? You may come to God as you would to your godfather, but if like your godfather God does not accept you, then what?"

Genesis 4.1–8 shows us how to come to God. If the way is wrong, you will not be able to approach Him. You may say you are showing Him a great honor. What if He rejects? It is a fact that sin is in the world, and this sin was committed by Adam. When Cain and Abel first came to God, they were both clean, for they had not committed any sin yet. Cain was a tiller of the ground, and he was an honest man. How did both of them come to God? Notice that in the garden of Eden it was God who sought man, not man after God. Outside the garden, however, it was a case of man seeking God. Neither of these two brothers was a man who had committed great and grave sins. They came to seek the presence of God. Yet to one of them (Cain) God declared that his way was wrong, and that therefore he could not come. But regarding Abel, we are told by the narrative that God accepted him because he brought a lamb slain.

The very fact that "in the sweat of thy face shalt thou eat bread" (Gen. 3.19) indicates that man is no longer in the garden of Eden. In the Edenic garden God would come to seek man, the grass would grow naturally, and the grains would ripen spontaneously. There was no need of fertilizers, and the produce was abundant. But now, in tilling the ground, a force is there to oppose man's wish, for the earth is under a curse.

Whether in farming or in politics or in education, everything betrays the fact that man is no longer in the garden of Eden. How can men who are now outside the garden use the same way of sacrificing as in the garden? How can they presume to believe and act as though nothing has happened? Without Christ, there is no way to come to God.

The question today is not how bad men are, but rather how dull they are. Suppose, for example, that a child is unhappy. He has broken not only a bowl but even the wok (a Chinese cooking pan). Yet after school he comes home as though nothing had ever happened. He might forget, but his parents cannot forget, for they were most disturbed by the careless attitude of their child. Let me say that Cain was in his day like this child. Both Cain and his brother Abel lived in a sinful world. It was not sufficient for them to come on the basis of their own works. They needed to come with the Lamb of God.

If man does not see original sin, sooner or later his own committed sins will spring forth. The Christian gospel tells us that we need Christ Jesus not only for our committed sins but also for our original sin. For we are no longer in the garden of Eden. Cain believed in God, and he wanted to worship God. But his sacrifice was wrong, and so he was rejected. We may not be as good as Cain; yet God is such a noble and holy God. We come with fear and trembling, yet God accepts us in His beloved Son.

4 | The Battle between the Old and the New

The most important thing after a believer is born again is to know how much he gains in regeneration as well as how much is left of his natural endowment. Such knowledge will help him to advance spiritually. Hence we intend to explain what is included in man's flesh, and how the Lord Jesus in His redemption deals with the various constituents of the flesh. In other words, our discussion together will tell us what we really obtain in regeneration.

"But I am carnal, sold under sin" (Rom. 7.14). "But sin which dwelleth in me . . . that is, in my flesh" (Rom. 7.17,18). By reading these two verses we know that the constituents of the flesh are "sin" and "I." The "sin" here is the power of sin, and the "I" here is what we commonly call the self. In order to appreciate spiritual life, we must not confuse these constituents of the flesh.

We know that the Lord Jesus has already dealt with our sin on the cross. The Scriptures tell us that "our old man was crucified with him" (Rom. 6.6). Nowhere in the Bible are we told to crucify ourselves, for this is what Christ has fully done, and that therefore there is no need for us to do anything. All we need to do is to reckon this fact to be true (see Rom. 6.11). Thus shall we experience the power of the death of Christ in setting us free from the power of sin (see Rom. 6.14).

Although the Bible never teaches us to crucify ourselves for the sake of sin, it does tell us to bear the cross for the sake of self. Many times our Lord Jesus commanded us to deny ourselves, take up the cross and follow Him. This is because the way in which our Lord deals with our self is different from the way in which He deals with our sins on the cross. We know that the Lord Jesus did not bear in His body our sins until He was on the cross, but He denied himself throughout His entire life without His having waited to do so until He reached the cross. For this reason, a believer may overcome sin completely in a matter of a second, but he needs to deny self all his life.

The letter to the Galatians explains clearly the two-sided relationship of the flesh to the believer. It tells us on the one hand: "they that are of Christ Jesus have crucified the flesh with the passions and the lusts thereof" (5.24). This means that on the day a person belongs to Christ Jesus his flesh is crucified. Unless he is taught by the Holy Spirit, he may conclude that he has no more flesh because it *was* crucified. Yet the Scriptures tell us on the other hand to "walk by the spirit, and ye shall not fulfill the lust of the flesh. For the flesh lusteth against the Spirit, and the Spirit against the flesh" (5.16,17). It is quite evident that a person who belongs to Christ Jesus and has the Holy Spirit indwelling him still has the flesh. He not only has the flesh, but also its power. Do these two passages contradict each other? Not at all. For verse 24 stresses the "sin" aspect of the flesh while verse 17 stresses the "self" aspect of the flesh. The cross of Christ deals with sin, and the Holy Spirit through the cross deals with the self. By the cross Christ delivers the believer from the power of sin so that sin reigns no more; by the Holy Spirit Christ dwells in the believer so that the latter may overcome his self. Overcoming sin is an accomplished fact; overcoming self is an affair being daily accomplished.

Were a believer to understand the perfect salvation of the cross at the time of his being born again—that is to say, when he receives the Lord Jesus as his Savior—he could overcome sin on the one hand, and receive a new life on the other. What is pitiable is that many workers do not present God's full salvation to a sinner, and thus what he believes and receives is only half of the complete salvation. His sins are forgiven, but he lacks the power not to sin again. Sometimes the salvation of God may be preached fully, yet the believer may obtain but half a salvation because he thinks only of the grace of forgiveness devoid of a sincere desire for the power to overcome sin.

But if a believer at the moment of regeneration believes and receives the full salvation of God, he will experience in his Christian life less of the defeats in fighting against sin and more of the battle with self. Unfortunately, however, such believers are rather scarce. Although we cannot count how many, we dare to say that there are not very many; on the contrary, the vast majority of believers only obtain half a salvation. Hence their battle is almost exclusively one engaged with sin. It is also possible that many at the time of their regeneration do not even know what the self is.

The experience of a person before his regeneration has also something to do with this area of concern. Many before their conversion had the tendency to do well (though they naturally did not have the power to do good). Although their conscience might have been more enlightened, their power to do good was minimal. Hence they experienced much struggling. This is what is commonly known as the battle between reason and lust. When such people hear the complete gospel, they most earnestly accept the grace of overcoming sin just as they previously received the grace of forgiveness. But with another class of people who—before their faith in Christ—were darkened in their conscience, had sinned greatly, and had never tried to do well, they most naturally seize upon the grace of forgiveness and neglect (not reject) the grace of overcoming sin at the time they hear the full salvation. Such people will have to experience more and more the battle with the sin of the flesh after their regeneration.

Why is this so? It is because as soon as a person is born again, he receives a new life which commands his obedience as well as demands his liberation from the rule of the flesh. For the life of God is absolute and it claims absolute authority. As soon as the divine life enters the spirit of man, it calls him to leave his former master, sin, and to yield completely to the Holy Spirit. But the sin in man is so deeply rooted, and the man's will—though it is partially renewed by the regenerated life—is still so joined with sin and self, that it still frequently inclines toward sin. So that the fierce battle between the new life and the flesh is unavoidable. Since such people are in the majority, we will speak more concerning their experience. However, I would remind the readers that such a prolonged struggle and defeats with sin (not with self) are really unnecessary.

What the flesh wants is total control, which is the very same desire of the spiritual life. The flesh wishes to put man permanently under it, whereas the spiritual life in man requires him to obey completely the Holy Spirit. The flesh and spiritual life are at odds at every point. The nature of the flesh is of the first man Adam, but that of the spiritual life is of the last Adam (Christ). The motive of the flesh is earthly, yet that of the spiritual is heavenly. The flesh makes self the center of all things, while the spiritual life centers all in Christ. Since these two are so radically different, it is no wonder that a believer finds a constant battle raging within him. The flesh tries to entice man to sin, but the spiritual life helps him to be righteous. A person who does not know the perfect salvation of Christ will experience much of this kind of battle after he is regenerated.

When young believers discover within themselves such a battle going on, they are truly dumbfounded. Some fall into despair, reckoning themselves as too corrupted to move ahead. Some even doubt their salvation. They do not see that they have such a battle within because of the very fact that they *are* born again. Formerly the flesh ruled without any interference. Though they committed many sins, they did not feel sinful, for their spirit was dead. Now, though, the new life has come and has brought with it many heavenly qualities, desires, lights, and concepts. As new light enters in, it exposes the uncleanness and corruption of the natural man. The new desire naturally abhors such prolonged uncleanness and corruption; and by contrast, it longs to do God's will. Thus the flesh fights against the spiritual life and vice versa. Such battling makes believers feel as though there are two persons within them: each has its own idea and power, and each strives for victory. If the spiritual life wins, believers experience much joy; if the flesh wins, they fall under accusation. Such experience actually proves that they have been born again.

God's purpose is not in reforming the flesh, but in destroying its vital center. In giving His life to man at the time of regeneration, God intends to use this life to destroy the self of the flesh. Although this life given by God to man is most powerful, in a new-born babe in Christ it is at first rather feeble. For the flesh has long held sway, and the newly born has not exercised faith to lay hold of God's perfect salvation. So that during this initial period, though he is born again, he is yet carnal. By carnality is meant that he is yet under the control of the flesh. What is most to be pitied is the fact that being born again, he already has the heavenly light shining in him. So he knows how wicked is the flesh and he desires with all his heart to overcome the flesh. But due to the feebleness of his inner strength, he cannot do what he wants to do. During this period he sheds many tears. In fact, every born-again child of God possesses this new desire of destroying sin in order to please God. Yet the will is not strong enough to overcome the flesh. Consequently, he experiences more defeats than he does victories. How deplorable is such a time!

The experience which Paul describes in Romans 7 is the history of such a battle:

> For that which I do I know not: for not what I would, that do I practise; but what I hate, that I do. . . . For I know that in me, that is, in my flesh, dwelleth no good thing: for to will is present with me, but to do that which is good is not. For the good which I would I do not: but the evil which I would not, that I practise. . . . I find then the law, that, to me who would do good, evil is present. For I delight in the law of God after the inward man: but I see a different law in my members, warring against the law of my mind, and bringing me into captivity under the law of sin which is in my members. (vv.15,18–19,21–23)

His final sigh is this: "Wretched man that I am! who shall deliver me out of the body of this death?" (v.24) How this sigh finds response in many hearts!

What does such battling really mean? Such battling is also a kind of discipline of the Holy Spirit. For God has already provided for man's perfect redemption. Man fails to obtain this so great salvation not because he does not know it but because he *wills* not to have it. God can only give it to those who believe it, receive it, and claim it singlemindedly for themselves. For this reason, when a person asks for forgiveness at the time of regeneration, he is given by God both forgiveness and regeneration. Then subsequently through such battling as we have already described, God induces a believer to seek and to lay hold of the *complete* victory in Christ. In case a believer fails to have victory due to the lack of knowledge, such struggling he experiences will urge him onward to seek to know, and the Holy Spirit will have the opportunity to reveal to him how Christ has already on the cross dealt with his old man, so that he will be led to believe and to possess. But if he *wills not* for such possession, the truth will remain in his mind until he discovers that knowledge alone will not help him in the battle. Many defeats may then eventually cause him to long to *experience* the truth he already knows.

Such battling will increase as the days go on. If a believer does not fall into despair, but advances forward faithfully, he will experience even *more* severe fightings. For such severe struggle will not cease until he finds deliverance. But deliverance will indeed come at last.

5 | The Reason for Believers' Defeats

> For that which I do I know not: for not what I would, that do I practise; but what I hate, that I do. (Rom. 7.15)
>
> There is therefore now no condemnation to them that are in Christ Jesus. For the law of the Spirit of life in Christ Jesus made me free from the law of sin and of death. (Rom. 8.1,2)

The children of God have a big problem: they are not able to live according to God's heart. Many profess that they are saved, and they are truly saved. But judging by the way they live, they are not in the garden of Eden. Salvation is complete, and the Promised Land is a land flowing with milk and honey. It is therefore imperative that we pay special attention to Romans 7, for this chapter will lead us to the realm of abundance.

Romans 3.23–25 tells us how a believer is justified through the redemption of the blood of Christ. Romans 6 shows us the relationship between the cross and me;

thus, I am made righteous. It enables us to know the effect of the cross. Strictly speaking, Romans 7 does not describe the battle betweeen the old life and the new life, nor does it recount the conflict of two natures. In reality, Romans 7 concerns itself with the fact that I am battling against myself: what I would, I do not; what I hate, I practice. The worst thing is that I become proud when I want to be humble and that I get angry when I want to be gentle. This indeed is the biggest battle in the world.

How, then, does Paul find out the secret of victory? Please notice especially two important words in Romans 7: (1) law, and (2) will. We see described here not a fight between the old life and the new, nor a battle between reason and lust, but a conflict between the will and the law. The conflict takes place not only in human lives, but also in the universe. Man exercises his will to battle against natural law. The law of gravity is a physical law. It is considered a law because it always acts the same way. An object will fall downward in Kweiyang as well as in Chungking. It is not affected by time or place. The power of gravity is to attract things downward to its center. If I refuse to release the object, I exercise my will to hold it up against the force of gravitation. At first the book I hold in my hand weighs two ounces, but gradually I feel the weight increasing to four pounds, and even to four tons if I could hold the book long enough. Finally I cannot stand it anymore. I have to give up. The law is inexhaustible, and consequently it always wins. The will always loses. This is true throughout the world. Since a law is not restricted by time or space, it exerts its force continuously.

In Romans 7 there is a great revelation concerning "sin." Sin is not simply an act, it is also a law. The reason why believers suffer repeated defeats is because they fail to know the nature of sin. For example, a sister once asked me, "I just do not understand why I am losing my temper today." From her words she seemed to be saying, "I am usually very good, but today I inadvertently lost my temper." She did not know that from God's viewpoint sin is a law. No doubt more sins will be committed by her.

Take the case of leprosy, for instance. When the appearance of the plague on a part of the skin is deeper than the skin of one's flesh, it is the plague of leprosy, and he shall be pronounced unclean. But if the leprosy covers all the skin of the one who has the plague, from his head even to his feet, he shall be pronounced clean (see Lev. 13). Why is this so? Because in spiritual terms the sinner — as typified by the leper — has finally come to the knowledge of what sin is. Sin is a law, not just an act. The realization of this brings in victory.

One day I discover that in me, that is, in my flesh, there is no good. I do not merely sin occasionally, I always sin. In Romans 7.21 Paul reveals a great discovery. "I *find* then the law, that, to me who would do good, evil is present." Through repeated failures, he falls upon a law. After we are saved, we have a new will. It is a great mistake to try to pitch our will against sin. What worries a preacher more than seeing people sin is seeing people try to do good. I may notice, for example, someone greatly attempting to be humble. I feel the pressure on him, for I know how very exhausting it must be for him to resist the law of sin with his will. Many Christians lose their joy in so doing. It is really hard work, and it ends up in the loss of joy. Why do they not find out the secret of overcoming the law? Their hard working has actually brought disgrace to the name of "Christian."

All who attempt to overcome sin by their will are wretched Christians. Suppose I am proud; what can I do about it? Shall I try to hold down my pride by exercising my will power? But will not my will wither just as my hand holding the book becomes numb? The victory which Christians claim in common is the *temporary* victory of the will. It is not a change of nature, nor does such victory originate with the Lord.

It is at that point that Paul lets out a sigh in Romans 7. If a Christian will sigh, blessed is he. How often we think we lose our temper because we have not controlled ourselves well. So we make a resolution to control ourselves better next time. But next time the same thing happens. After a defeat, the first thought which comes to our mind is that we have not resisted enough. Let us clearly understand, however, that this thought is entirely wrong. Because overcoming sin by the will is only temporary victory and is changeable. The law of sin, though, is permanent and unchangeable.

We read in Romans 8.1 that "there is therefore now no condemnation to them that are in Christ Jesus." "No condemnation" can be translated as "not without strength." The law of the Spirit of life which God gives overcomes with its greater strength the law of sin and of death. The problem here is not conduct; for God delivers us not only from a sin but also from the *law* of sin and of death. Simply put, God uses another law to deal with this law. It is not the will, but one law pitted against another law. Iron will fall to the ground. This is according to the law of gravity. But another law—that of magnetism—can keep the iron from falling.

Does the law of the Spirit of life dwell in you? Each life has its own law. Simply speaking, law is habit. After I am saved, I not only have obtained life, but also *the habit* of this new life. Let me illustrate it this way: A fish has its life, and its constant law is to swim in the water. A living life must have its law. No fish with a fish life can merely float but not swim as well. If it is a fish, it swims. For where life is, there is law; and vice versa. Again, a bird has its life, and flying is its law. It is a basic error to think that one can receive a bird's life but must then learn how to fly. For if one cannot fly, his is not a bird's life.

When God gives us new life, He also gives us the *law* of the Spirit of life. He gives us *habits* as well as life. This is called regeneration. The characteristic of a Christian lies in the fact that God gives us a special law at the time He gives us new life. It is effortless for a believer to do good. It is merely following the nature of the life received. God's life in you will cause you to follow Him. Since the Lord has borne my all on the cross, will He desert me now? Using the same example of the power of gravity, your Bible will not fall to the ground if it is placed on a table. Another law is working against the book to keep it from falling. You do not need to support the Bible with your hand with all your strength. If you know that you have the *law* of the Spirit of life in you, you can declare, as Paul does, that "there is therefore now no condemnation."

It was discovered in 1884 in an old manuscript found in Egypt that the Greek word for "condemnation" has two different interpretations: one carries within it a legal connotation, and the other a civil connotation. In legal terms it is translated as condemnation; in civil terms it is translated as strengthlessness or limitation. In Christ Jesus you are no longer without strength or limited.

In reading Romans 7, you find how wretched is the fact that you cannot do what you will to do. In reading Romans 8, however, you discover a new gospel is being announced. The issue is whether or not it will be law against law. If you meet temptation, then use this secret and you will overcome. For God is well able to deal with any temptation you may face.

Once a widow lost her son of twenty-three years old. The telephone rang, calling her to go to gather the dead body. She knelt down and prayed, "O Lord, unless You bring me through, I can never get through." Sure enough, God brought her through. She was delivered from agony.

A bird will say it is most easy to fly, but most difficult to swim. A Christian should be able to say it is most easy to overcome, but very hard to sin. Amen!

6 | Faith

We notice in the Bible that what God requires of His children is faith. Without faith, it is impossible to be well-pleasing to God (Heb. 11.6). Every spiritual blessing as well as every arrangement of special circumstances is obtained through faith. It really amazes us when we think of how much God stresses the faith of the believer. The perfect salvation as presented in the Bible seems to be nearly always experienced by faith.

One thing is quite evident from Scripture: that God hates the works of the wicked. Whatever comes out of self, be it from sinner or saint; whatever can be done without trusting God but done with one's own idea and strength — it is hated by God. In spite of the fact that many things look good in human eyes, they are nevertheless rejected by God. The Lord Jesus himself tells us that "there is [one] who is good" (Matt. 19.17), and this One is God. According to the view of Christ, none other is good. Hence all which is not done according to the will of the God who is good and by God's strength is not good but is all sinful. For there is no one good except God. Nothing outside of His will and power is good. All the works of the believer must therefore be of God and through God.

Now it is just here that this issue of faith enters into the picture. Faith is composed of two basic principles: (1) To cease from man's own work, and (2) to wait for God to work. Ordinarily we consider faith as trusting, depending and waiting for God to work; not realizing that there is the prerequisite of ceasing our own work first. To cease from man's own work is reckoned as a work of faith. Waiting for God to work happens in the believer's heart, hence it is invisible; but ceasing from one's own work is external, therefore it may sometimes be seen. The greater work of faith is manifested in the believer ceasing from his own work rather than in waiting for God to work for him.

The importance of such a step cannot be overemphasized. For God is never willing to mix His own work in with the work of man's flesh. What God requires of the believer is to cease from all that is of his own self, including his idea and strength. No doubt God is pleased to be trusted and relied upon by the believer. But how is such faith in God expressed? By being still and completely resting from one's self. This is the first step in the work of faith.

Where can you find a man who is still busily plotting and working after he has fully trusted his friend? If God is trustworthy and His power is sufficiently great, will He need our help? If we believe God will work for us, is there any room for worrying? Are we afraid that He may not be able to do it well? Such attitudes prove that we do not really believe. Faith demands us to be fully rested: neither worrying in heart nor laboring in body. If we have no rest in body as well as in heart — that is to say, if we are yet laboring and worrying — we show ourselves to be people without faith.

Hence the first principle of faith is to cease from our own works. Should we continue to worry over our petty self and our difficult environment, how can we say that we have looked upon God? If we are still engaged in toil by means of our own talents, strength, relationship and maneuver, can we possibly claim that we know how useless we are and that we have therefore committed all matters into the hand of God? The life of faith is a life of self-denial. The work of faith is a self-denying work. Faith calls us to forsake our petty self with its insignificant worrying, as well as to forsake our own strength together with its laboring. To cease completely from one's own labor is the first manifestation of the work of faith.

Strange to say, however, a believer does not naturally possess this kind of faith. As the faith at the time of regeneration was given to us by God (see Eph. 2.8), so the faith for our daily living must also be given by Him. To prove how useless is the believer himself, it is sufficient to mention that he has absolutely no faith even to believe unless it is received from God. All faith is given by God. The faith which the apostle Paul lists among the gifts of the Holy Spirit is likewise a gift given by God (see 1 Cor. 12.9a).

Are there not times when we would like very much to believe in God and to commit our affairs wholly to

Him? We have been exhorted to exercise our faith to trust in God, but no matter how much we exercise, we simply cannot trust. There are times when we exercise so vigorously as though our heart is ready to burst; yet the faith we manufacture is ineffective. We have gathered up all our strength to fight against doubt, and still we do not attain our goal. Such a condition is indeed most painful. What anguish a believer experiences in wrestling against doubt!

But this is not faith. For faith is not something that man can stir up or manufacture or bring out from his own heart. Faith must be given by God. It is this God-given faith that governs the believer, not the believer who manages this faith. Frequently we desire to have faith to accomplish a certain task, but where can we go to find this faith? Many times we have neither desire nor idea in ourselves, yet God gives us faith to be expressed through prayer which brings in great success.

God does not give us faith that we might fulfill our own desire. Our proper place is death, which is, to prostrate ourselves in dust and ashes. Acccording to God's will, a saint lives on earth for the Lord's will and glory alone. It is not legitimate for him to decide what he wants or does. God desires to use us as His vessels, but this calls for our death. In accomplishing a work by trusting in God, we are merely being used as a vessel. God desires to accomplish something, so He gives us faith that we may pray and ask Him to work, and then He works till that which He wills is done. Naturally the flesh feels uncomfortable about it, because it does not give the flesh any chance to maneuver nor any ground to obtain its desire. Yet a believer who truly lives for God and not for himself will joyfully be a dead instrument in order to fulfill God's highest will.

See how 'wise is our God! For if faith were something we ourselves had and it came out from us, why, we would then become its master. Whenever we wanted to do a particular thing, we would only need to believe and we would have God to work it out for us. But this is not so. Faith is something given by God. Before He gives us faith, we just cannot believe. Many of us Christians share in the experience of frequently finding no way to enter into rest because we simply are unable to manufacture faith. Then suddenly God gives faith (sometimes it comes through one or two scripture passages; sometimes it comes after prayer when we know intuitively the will of God), and our heart immediately calms down and enters into rest, as if a kind of assurance has been given to us that God will do the work. Such faith comes naturally without the need of struggling, anxiety, and exercise. As soon as God grants faith, the believer instantly exhibits the work of faith, which is rest without worrying. Whatever is humanly manufactured is not faith, and therefore does not give rest.

A word of cautionary discernment is necessary at this point. For what has been mentioned above does not mean that now we have no other responsibility but to wait for faith to come. Faith actually may be divided into two kinds: the special and the ordinary. Special faith is given to us by God concerning some particular matter, thus enabling us to believe that God will accomplish it for us. Such special faith does not happen on every occasion.

Ordinary faith is the faith which an experienced believer *always* has towards God. It is not directed at a particular matter, but rather towards *all* matters. Such faith assumes the believing attitude that *whatever* God does is *right*. Failure or success is all within the perfect will of God. Although we have special faith only occasionally, we ought to have ordinary faith towards all things which come our way, believing our God can do no wrong, trusting that everything is in His hands, and acknowledging He knows what is best for us, whether suffering or success. We should have this ordinary faith at all times. Even when special things happen, we must not lose this kind of faith.

In any case, whatever kind of faith it may be, it must be manifested in work. This is to say, that it must give the believing one rest from laboring with his natural strength to help God.

7 | The Condition for Spiritual Growth

Now there cried a certain woman of the wives of the sons of the prophets unto Elisha, saying, Thy servant my husband is dead; and thou knowest that thy servant did fear Jehovah: and the creditor is come to take unto him my two children to be bondmen. And Elisha said unto her, What shall I do for thee? tell me; what hast thou in the house? And she said, Thy handmaid hath not anything in the house, save a pot of oil. Then he said, Go, borrow thee vessels abroad of all thy neighbors, even empty vessels; borrow not a few. And thou shalt go in, and shut the door upon thee and upon thy sons, and pour out into all those vessels; and thou shalt set aside that which is full. So she went from him, and shut the door upon her and upon her sons; they brought the vessels to her, and she poured out. And it came to pass, when the vessels were full, that she said unto her son, Bring me yet a vessel. And he said unto her, There is not a vessel more. And the oil stayed. (2 Kings 4.1–6)

Blessed are they that hunger and thirst after righteousness: for they shall be filled. (Matt. 5.6)

The hungry he hath filled with good things; and the rich he hath sent empty away. (Luke 1.53)

The Reasons for Not Growing

The reasons for a believer's failure and lack of growth are: (1) not knowing himself; and (2) not knowing the riches of the Lord. An unknown Christian at the famed Keswick Convention once declared that the defeat of the believer is due to these two reasons.

The One Condition for Growth

The only condition for being blessed by God resulting in spiritual growth or in experiencing the riches of the Lord is self-emptying. We should always empty ourselves. The hungry alone shall be filled with good things. All the spiritual grace of God is for the hungry.

The procedure of the operation of the Holy Spirit in us is first to create in us a longing, causing us to be dissatisfied with our current life; for the start of retrogression in one's spiritual life is satisfaction, whereas the commencement of progress is *dis*satisfaction. The Holy Spirit does the work of emptying before He does the work of filling. God hollows us out in order to then fill us. Hollowing out is God's means, but filling up is God's end. For the purpose of emptying us, the Holy Spirit will allow us to meet difficulties. All these difficulties are arranged by the Holy Spirit to lead us to deeper seeking. The victory at Jericho cannot be used to fight against the next and smaller city of Ai. We cannot use yesterday's huge victory to fight today's small battle. Past experience is not sufficient for present need. God never asks us to eat yesterday's manna.

Thank God, we have problems! Through the Holy Spirit God creates problems for us in our life and environment. He allows us to try to meet present problems with our past experience, thus incurring defeat. Yet with the defeat comes a desire, a new desire. For faith never tries to imitate the past. We cannot imitate the works of faith according to the likeness of the past, though we *can* imitate other believers' faith. Having already observed the Lord feeding the five thousand with five loaves and shortly afterwards the four thousand with seven loaves, the disciples ought to have known better. Even without *any* loaf, the Lord would be able to feed them. Yet on a later occasion they reasoned one with another, saying: "We have no bread" (Mark 8.16), because they did not know the Lord better. So God orders our environment in order to lead us to a deeper knowledge of himself as well as a deeper knowledge of ourselves and our emptiness. He lets us fail that we may know our emptiness and uselessness. You and I as natural men must be crossed out by God on the cross.

The Way to Be Filled

According to the record of 2 Kings 4.1–6, three things mentioned there in connection with the filling of oil can provide us with three fundamental principles for being filled and thus experiencing spiritual growth:

(1) *Prepare empty vessels*. The widow was in debt

because of the poverty of her husband. What she had was only a pot of oil. This pot was basic and essential to the repaying of her debt and to the supporting of her life. All that she lacked now were empty vessels. So Elisha advised her to borrow quite a few empty vessels. In our own case, because of Adam, we too became poor. But thank God, we have the Holy Spirit. What we lack are empty rooms for the Holy Spirit to fill. Not that we cannot be filled, only that we have no empty rooms for the Holy Spirit to work. For the Holy Spirit only fills vacuums. To make spiritual progress, we need always to be empty so that we may always be filled. It is not that we are once emptied and forever filled. Not so. Again and again, we need more emptiness and more filling.

(2) *Shut the door.* Have dealings with the Holy Spirit in secret, in the hidden place. Shut out the flesh and shut in the Holy Spirit. Whenever we encounter difficulty, we should deal with the Holy Spirit in the secret place. This will solve our problem in life.

(3) *The oil stays when there is no more empty vessel.* The filling stops because there is no more emptiness. If the emptiness is unlimited, the filling will be boundless. Esau was the first self-satisfied person, therefore he ended up as the first empty person. We ought to be emptied continuously, not just emptied once. We must always be emptied that we may always be filled. *We* are responsible for *emptiness*, while the *Holy Spirit* is responsible for *filling*.

8 | The Condescension of the Lord Jesus

Only the Highest can condescend to be the lowest. Throughout the life of our Lord, we may notice how He condescends himself all around. As we read the four Gospels, we can truly see a condescending life portrayed before us. This constitutes one of the reasons for our admiration and worship of Him. Naturally His condescension touches many areas, but the most beautiful is seen in His working together with the created beings and His using them as His instrument.

He is the Creator who "calleth the things that are not, as though they were" (Rom. 4.17). Speak a word, and the thing is done. His word is absolute and infinite. His word is backed up by His authority and power. Hence whatever He says is accomplished. He has no need of helpers or of raw materials with which to work. His authority and power are sufficient for all accomplishments. The Creator is in no need of co-workers or instruments.

Yet how amazing were His actions on earth! He used

the seven loaves and a few fish offered to him by His disciples to feed the four thousand. If He could feed such a multitude with such a little amount of bread and fish, surely He could also create some bread and fish to feed them all. Such a creative act would not be cumbersome for Him. He is able to perform miracles, any kind of miracle. Whether to call something into being out of nothing or to multiply what is already at hand is something equally easy for Him to do. Nevertheless, He condescends himself and takes pleasure to share His work and glory with His disciples.

He loves to draw His people into the thing which He is going to do. He is not willing to be independent. He does not want to do everything by himself alone. He is delighted to have His people work with Him. For it is His pleasure to see His own partake in His work. He likes to bring the created into the work of the Creator. He loves to let them know how He will use them and what is theirs by which to manifest His glory in their lives if they are willing to offer, to obey, and to trust Him. How glorious and how condescending! He always appreciates the union of His people with himself.

As He was about to enter Jerusalem, He could very well have exercised His creative power to create an ass for His ride through the city—just as He had created many living creatures during the time when, according to Genesis 1.1–2ff., He repaired the earth. And yet He took pleasure in sending His disciples to fetch the ass with the colt by saying, "The Lord hath need of them" (Matt. 21.3). Could it be true that the Lord of creation is in lack and has need? But He himself said it. He knew beforehand that in yonder village an ass with its colt were tied there; He also foreknew that no man had ever sat on that colt. He knew what question the owner of the ass would ask when His disciples loosed them. He knew as well the owner would let them take the ass and the colt if they answered in a certain way. All this is indeed miraculous. Our Lord would rather perform His miracle in this way than create an ass miraculously without either using their ass or sending His disciples on the errand. This is His condescension. He could with one word create an ass colt a hundred times better than any colt then existing in the world, yet He delights in receiving human help.

May I reverently say this: that He desired some contributions from men while on His earthly pilgrimage. He loved to make men His companions. He was willing to receive whatever help towards His work from the hands of those who loved and honored Him. No doubt He could have proceeded alone without using any man; but He disliked that way. He took great joy in condescendingly receiving a little contribution from man. How He today delights to uplift man by letting him have a part in His work!

"The Lord hath need of him [or, The Lord is in lack of him]" (Luke 19.31). Did He mean to say that His lack could not be supplied if this owner refused to offer the colt to Him? He now had a need; He loved to let man fulfill His need. He would rather receive from the hand of His people that supply towards His need rather than to fill in by performing a miracle alone. If His people would faithfully offer, He would then ride on their colt to enter Jerusalem and accept the hosannas from the multitudes. If the believers were lazy or stingy, He would rather wait and let His need stand long unfulfilled. He refuses to exercise His divine power to do the work. He is never in haste. For this is His will. He loves to act this way. Though we do not know why, yet we know He loves this way. Whoever understands the Lord's heart ought to see his responsibility here.

By acting in the way just described, the Lord condescends himself on the one hand and uplifts us on the other. We wonder if we are worthy of such exaltation: that the created has the opportunity of supplying the need of the Creator—if this is not elevating, what then is it? With this thought in mind, our murmurings would be greatly lessened when we are moved by the Holy Spirit to offer.

What a terrible mistake for any of us to think that we are being gracious to God, and that we are therefore meritorious before Him when we offer ourselves and what is ours to Him. The truth is that God, in desiring our offerings and being willing to accept them, actually elevates us and glorifies us. God being honorable beyond compare, with the heavenly angels as His servants and possessing the cattle on a thousand hills and all the gold and silver on earth—can He truly be in lack? Would He ever need the power and materials of such poor and humble people as we are? Is He really at His wit's end that He asks help from us? Or is it instead that He uses this need to elevate and uplift us, letting us know that however base and lowly we are, we are given the privilege of supplying His need and rushing to His help. This is too wonderful indeed!

Is it not amazing that God is willing to accept our

power and property? It would be astonishing for a king to accept anything of a beggar. Does he really have no other means but what the beggar supplies? Or does the king have some other purpose in mind? For the beggar to have the opportunity of helping his king, how would he feel—honored or virtuous? But to offer to *our* King is our unexpected privilege.

Let all believers know and understand that for such insignificant beings as we are to have the opportunity to forsake something for, or to offer something to, God is our high and special privilege. It will be our great honor if He is willing to accept us, but what an even greater honor that he even asks us! Due to the dullness of our heart in failing to realize the great honor in being able to make such an offering, we sometimes boast of our suffering, forsaking, and sacrificial giving to the Lord as though *we* have been benevolent to *Him*! Alas, we just do not understand how He has honored us! Had we understood, we would not be so hesitating and considering at such great length when it comes to our service to the Lord. Moreover, we would not lay up for ourselves treasures upon the earth, nor would we consider a tiny offering as being such a big honor to the Lord.

The word of Mordecai is most fitting here. "If thou altogether holdest thy peace at this time," he said to Queen Esther, "then will relief and deliverance arise to the Jews from another place, . . . and who knoweth whether thou art not come to the kingdom for such a time as this?" (Esther 4.14) The people of God today have many lacks, and God looks at these as His own lacks. He wishes to fill these lacks, but He will not perform miracles by himself to solve these needs. He wants to use you. Are you willing?

God is well able to send His angel to proclaim His word from heaven to revive His people. He is well able to show from heaven many signs and wonders to awaken the sinners of the world. And He is also well able to shower manna from heaven to support all His servants and maids who look to Him for their subsistence. But if He should do these things, you would lose your glory and your participation in God's work. He will indeed perform a miracle to deliver, but He loves to do it through you and me, for He has no desire to do it alone. How He is willing to condescend himself, how He delights to elevate us. He enjoys to have us participate in all His works. He is so humble to say, "I have need." Yet this is to open a door for us to render Him service and to gain His glory. Such being the case, why not offer ourselves to the Lord? Why not offer our material goods? How foolish of us if we do not know how to buy up the timely opportunity.

To sum up, then. In God's work of saving people, He looks for men to work with Him. If you do not respond, He will raise up others in your stead. In His work of building up the believers, He also needs men. If you draw back, He will raise up others as substitutes for you. God gives you wealth in order that you may supply the need of His work. If you fail, He will raise up others. God's needs must be filled; what only remains is, who will fill them, who will preach the word, who will fulfill God's glory? Suppose you do not respond. Do not think that God is now totally helpless. He will raise up other people. Yet what is to be pitied is that you lose this portion of glory: "if thou altogether holdest thy peace at this time, then will relief and deliverance arise to the Jews from another place." Therefore, let "no one take thy crown" (Rev. 3.11).

God's need today may be said to be greater than those at any other time. This is because He wants to give special glory to the believers of this age. He is still willing to condescend himself. But will believers today humbly and thankfully supply God's current need, marvel at His grace, and take it as their unsurpassing honor?

9 | The Helpmeet of Christ

And Jehovah God said, It is not good that the man
should be alone; I will make him a helpmeet for him. And
out of the ground Jehovah God formed every beast of
the field, and every bird of the heavens; and brought them
unto the man to see what he should call them: and whatsoever the man called every living creature, that was the
name thereof. And the man gave names to all cattle, and
to the birds of the heavens, and to every beast of the field;
but for man there was not found a helpmeet for him. And
Jehovah God caused a deep sleep to fall upon the man,
and he slept; and he took one of his ribs, and closed up
the flesh instead thereof: and the rib, which Jehovah God
had taken from the man, made he a woman, and brought
her unto the man. And the man said, This is now bone
of my bones, and flesh of my flesh: she shall be called
Woman, because she was taken out of Man. (Gen. 2.18-23)

In this passage of the Scriptures, there are two types

presented: Adam as a type of Christ, and Eve as a type of the church (see Eph. 5.31,32). Ephesians 5.25-29 speaks of this kind of relationship between the believer and Christ; while Genesis 2.18-23 speaks of the kind of relationship between the believer and God.

From this passage in Genesis 2, we may see how different is the thought of God from the thought of man. It was not man but God who said, "It is not good that the man should be alone."

That which the Bible emphasizes is what God says. When we expect sinners to be saved, we contemplate the benefit to the sinners; for unless they repent they will perish and suffer, but if they believe in the Lord Jesus, they may have eternal life. According to Genesis 2.18-23, however, God's chief thought is for Christ, not man. Sinners saved are God's gift to Christ, even as Jesus in John 17.6 states in His prayer to the Father: "the men whom thou gavest me out of the world." God not only gives Christ to men, He also gives men to Christ. The special gift which God gives to Christ are the sinners. God does this to satisfy the heart of Christ.

The one great purpose of a believer on earth is to live for Christ. Adam was not made for Eve, but Eve was made for Adam. Hence believers are made for Christ; therefore, we ought to give satisfaction to Christ.

In the Bible there are two marriages mentioned which may express both the direct relationship of Christ and the church and the indirect relationship of God giving the church to Christ. These two marriages are that of Rebecca to Isaac and that of Rachel to Jacob through his service to Laban. In the first case, we learn that Isaac did not know Rebecca; instead, his father Abraham arranged the marriage. In the second case, Jacob married Rachel through his own suffering. Suppose Rebecca proved to be a poor match; Isaac could then blame his father since the maiden was chosen by his father. We know in fact, however, that Abraham arranged a marriage which brought great satisfaction to his son. This serves as a type of how God chooses the church for Christ and how God gives Christ great satisfaction. Even though Rachel was not so pure in character, but rather jealous at times, Jacob had no complaint because he loved Rachel with all his heart, and he had willingly suffered much for her. Thus the relationship of Christ to the church is like the marriage of Jacob to Rachel; and the relationship of God to the church is like the marriage which Abraham arranged for his son Isaac with Rebecca. The church comes to Christ through the hand of God. This is what we want to present here: that even as Rebecca was given by Abraham to his son Isaac, so the church has been given by the Father to His beloved Son.

In God's mind, Christ does not seem to be complete without us. It is not good for Christ to be alone. He will appear to be lacking without gaining sinners such as we. So that the purpose of God in saving us is not just for our sake, it is for the sake of Christ as well. God wants His Christ to be satisfied, happy and complete; therefore He gives us to Christ. May we see that we are called not merely to obtain personal blessings, but much more to satisfy the heart of Christ.

We have a responsibility not to fail God's purpose.

If we learn to satisfy Christ, then we are cooperating with God in His great purpose.

There are two places in the Bible that contain the phrase, "shall be satisfied." One of these refers to how Christ "shall see of the travail of his soul, and shall be satisfied (Is. 53.11); the other has reference to the believers themselves: "I shall be satisfied, when I awake [at the time of resurrection], with beholding thy form" (Ps. 17.15). May we satisfy His heart.

We should save sinners because life begets life. Because God is life, He creates and redeems men so that they may have the same life. But let us never forget that all this is for Christ, His beloved Son.

TITLES YOU
WILL WANT TO HAVE

by Watchman Nee

by Stephen Kaung

ORDER FROM:

Christian Fellowship Publishers, Inc.
11515 Allecingie Parkway
Richmond, Virginia 23235